PRAISE FOR
LEARNING ANALYTICS

'If you need to evaluate your investments in talent, or use HR analytics to inform business decisions, then this book is a godsend. In today's talent economy, *Learning Analytics* is a small investment with a high return. Adopt these findings so that you can attract, develop and retain your desired employees.'
Doug Gray, CEO, Action Learning Associates, and President, Nashville ATD

'John, Jean and Mark start where others stop. The point is that analytics is more than just ROI calculations. Three key points are: first, the game belongs to prediction. You can't change the past, but you can learn how to apply it in predictive methods. Second, data integration generates leverage. This implies that development professionals have to be keen students of the workings and purposes of their organizations. Third, it's all about application. We can't just dump findings on management. We have to be partners in using the outcomes to run the organizations more effectively. The authors do a great job of leading the reader through these points.'
Dr Jac Fitz-enz, Founder, Saratoga Institute, and author of over a dozen books on human capital

'You don't need to be a statistical guru to find value in this book. While there are statistical examples, this book really addresses the value that's realized by applying analytics to learning and development programmes. John, Jean and Mark have combined decades of research and experience to create a clear and compelling read about using learning data to speak the language of business leaders.'
Kristin Colber-Baker, Director, Global Programs and Learning Measurement, Mars University, Mars, Inc

'*Learning Analytics* takes a brave aspiration – everything you ever needed to know about how to measure organizational learning – and encapsulates the best industry guidance into nine compelling chapters. This book outlines how to stop operating on anecdotes and start functioning with evidence. It also provides answers to objections that have stalled our field for years with its pragmatic models, how-tos, research and case studies. This is truly an exceptional read and a gift to the learning and talent field at large.'
Kieran King, Global Vice President, Customer Insight at Skillsoft

'To quote Sun Tzu: "Know yourself and you will win all battles"! Data, when handled skilfully, provides a rich stream of actionable information that enables smart business decisions. This book shows us how to accomplish just that, and is a must-have reference for anyone in the business of learning. The authors are trailblazers in the field of analytics, and provide practical steps that stakeholders can take to ensure their evaluation dollars are spent wisely. More importantly, they focus first and foremost on how to align future learning programmes with the needs of the business, which directly impacts programme funding and executive sponsorship. Full of case studies and real-life examples to illustrate best practices, this book brings the latest thinking in the ever-emerging field of talent management analytics.'
Andy Wainwright, Vice President, HR Partnerships at CareerCurve

'*Learning Analytics* moves beyond the standard approaches to evaluation. It emphasizes the role that technology plays to make the evaluation process more efficient for large-scale organizations and more insightful for end-users of the data.'
Kimo Kippen, Chief Learning Officer, Hilton Worldwide

Learning Analytics

Measurement innovations to
support employee development

John R Mattox II and Mark Van Buren
with insights from Jean Martin

Publisher's note

Every possible effort has been made to ensure that the information contained in this book is accurate at the time of going to press, and the publishers and authors cannot accept responsibility for any errors or omissions, however caused. No responsibility for loss or damage occasioned to any person acting, or refraining from action, as a result of the material in this publication can be accepted by the editor, the publisher or the author.

First published in Great Britain and the United States in 2016 by Kogan Page Limited

2nd Floor, 45 Gee Street
London
EC1V 3RS
United Kingdom

1518 Walnut Street
Suite 900
Philadelphia PA 19102
USA

4737/23 Ansari Road
Daryaganj
New Delhi 110002
India

www.koganpage.com

© John R Mattox II, Mark Van Buren and Jean Martin, 2016

ISBN   978 0 7494 7630 4
E-ISBN   978 0 7494 7636 6

British Library Cataloguing-in-Publication Data

A CIP record for this book is available from the British Library.

Library of Congress Cataloging-in-Publication Control Number

2016029321

Typeset by Graphicraft Limited, Hong Kong
Print production managed by Jellyfish
Printed and bound by CPI Group (UK) Ltd, Croydon CR0 4YY

References to websites (URLs) were accurate at the time of writing. Neither the authors nor Kogan Page is responsible for URLs that may have expired since the manuscript was prepared.

I wish to thank my family and colleagues for all of your support in writing this book.
John R Mattox II

My deepest thanks to the many learning and development professionals and leaders who continue to advance the profession, and to my family – Shari, Andrew, Stephen and Matthew – for their constant support and encouragement.
Mark Van Buren

For Warren, Caleb, Tess and Josh, and for all the many distinguished leaders of human resources and learning and development we are privileged to serve and to be inspired by.
Jean Martin

CONTENTS

FOREWORD

Approximately 80 books have been written in the United States on the evaluation of learning. We were fortunate to have authored the first one, *Handbook of Training Evaluation and Measurement Methods*, published by Gulf Publishing in 1983, and the most recent one, *Real World Training Evaluation*, published by ATD in 2016. When considering this number of books on a single topic, a question comes to mind: 'Do we need another book on the measurement, evaluation and analytics of the learning profession?' Our response: Yes!

Complex and persistent problems require multiple solutions to address them properly. Demonstrating the value of learning investments consists of several such problems, and many practitioners do not fully understand why they linger. The different audiences with an interest in addressing these problems require multiple solutions with a variety of techniques, approaches and models – all aimed at motivating practitioners to step up to the challenge.

Learning is a precious activity. It is central to building organization capability, driving operational excellence, building customer relationships, and ensuring innovative and sustainable performance. It is through learning that organizations advance from good to great. It is through learning that organizations achieve outstanding results, and it doesn't stop with organizations. Our communities, states and nations are by-products of learning – whether learning occurs individually, collectively, or collaboratively. Executives will invest more in learning when we fully understand how to measure and optimize its value. This book is another valuable solution to our need to show value in learning.

What are the problems?

The problems with the investment in learning rest within five major issues. These are not new concerns, and we are making progress, but the issues persist.

1 Learning is rarely measured at the levels desired by the executives in the organization

Several studies now clearly show that executives want to see the business connection from learning, whether the organization is a business, government, nonprofit, or non-governmental organization. The good news is that it is possible to achieve this, and this book will help.

2 Most learning has an inappropriate beginning

It is rare for learning to align to the business at inception. This is unfortunate because the business connection should be the starting point of any investment. Some learning teams understand this and approach learning with business needs in mind: most do not. Additionally, learning is frequently the proposed solution, when in many cases it is not the right solution. Other solutions could be much better. On some occasions, learning is the absolute wrong solution, and sometimes, when learning is the right solution, it is often subpar. This book will help with this issue.

3 Much of learning is wasted

We hear a lot about scrap learning: the part of learning that is wasted when learning programmes are implemented. Waste occurs when someone has learned knowledge or skills that should be used on the job, but does not apply them. Research suggests that waste can range from 60 to 90 per cent of the learning. While we are making some progress in this area, much more is needed. This book will help.

4 Learning and development professionals are not prepared to tackle these issues appropriately

Whether they landed their jobs through academic preparation or rotational assignment, the vast majority of L&D team members have no formal preparation for evaluation, measurement, analytics, or ROI. This is changing, although not fast enough. This book will help.

5 Learning and development professionals are not motivated to pursue evaluation

Evaluation duties are not restricted to those individuals who have full-time evaluation responsibilities. Evaluation is the responsibility of all stakeholders. When evaluation is not your full-time job, it is easy to let other activities get in the way. The other tasks are all the things that we really like to do. We don't pursue evaluation because we perceive it as too complex, too confusing, too difficult, and we are not sure we really need it. As Pogo, the cartoon character, so appropriately said, 'We have met the enemy, and he is us.' This book will help to motivate the team to pursue evaluation.

What's needed

Important changes are needed in our learning systems. These are not new issues. Seasoned professionals have been discussing these issues in some way or another for years. But they can be addressed following these simple steps:

1 Start with 'Why?'

The beginning of a learning solution should be a business measure that represents why we are implementing the solution. The 'Why' shows all stakeholders the reason for the programme or solution. Stakeholders should not have to wonder why they are investing in a learning solution. We recommend that there should be at least some level of discussion about the business need for every programme. Some organizations have taken this to the extreme by not allowing a programme to be developed unless the business measure is identified and an objective is written to describe the impact it will deliver. For example, Jenny Dearborn, Chief Learning Officer for SAP, speaking at an ATD conference last year, indicated that SAP has made this shift. Unfortunately, most organizations have not.

2 Think measurement in the beginning

The ADDIE (analysis, design, development, implementation and evaluation) model, where evaluation is usually stuck at the end, often creates the illusion that evaluation is only a concern when it is all over – we do it if we have to. Unfortunately, evaluation needs to be addressed early and often, from the initial analysis and through every phase of the process so that opportunities for adjustments are evident. Also, processes must exist to drive the desired results and create expectations for those results. If we think about measurement only at the end, we are at a disadvantage. For example, just this week, the head of learning and development for one of the government agencies of Saudi Arabia told us that he was asked to show the impact of learning programmes within two weeks, otherwise the programmes would be cut. Unfortunately, this person has no data showing the value of any of these programmes. This crisis could have been avoided had he considered measurement at the beginning. This situation may be extreme, but unfortunately, it occurs far too often.

3 **Take measurement beyond the classroom, the keyboard, or the mobile device**

There is a lingering perception that we can only measure what we can control. We control the learning when the learner is captive. We can force them to provide data and measure their success with learning. Unfortunately, if they do not use what they have learned, then the learning is wasted, and the programme that we thought was successful is now considered a failure. Push the evaluations to Level 3 Application, Level 4 Impact, and, yes, occasionally, Level 5 ROI. The data at these levels, while more challenging to capture, tells the real story about the value of the learning investment.

4 **Focus on process improvement, not performance evaluation for any stakeholder group**

One of the greatest barriers to more evaluation is the fear of the outcomes. If a programme is not working, the owners of the programme may not want to see the results if they are negative. After all, they have supported, designed, facilitated and implemented the programme. Because of this, we must approach evaluation from the perspective of process improvement – improving the programme, not the individuals. If we approach evaluation this way, we stand a much better chance of collecting credible data, gaining acceptance for adjustments and taking some of the fear out of negative results that may be present at some point.

5 Manage measurement and evaluation resources

No organization has an unlimited budget, and when money is allocated to measurement and evaluation, it is taking away from design, development and delivery. All of these functions are important. Unfortunately, we have underinvested in measurement and evaluation, averaging around 1 per cent of the learning budget for most organizations. Best practice is in the 3 to 5 per cent range, but even then, that's a lot of money for some large organizations. If we are not careful, we can spend more than we need to. This book will help readers manage their resources, particularly when using technology to keep the investment in measurement, evaluation and analytics at a reasonable amount, suitable for most budgets.

6 Share the joy

Measurement, evaluation and analytics are not just for those who have evaluation or analytics in their job title. It is everyone's responsibility, including analysts, designers, developers, facilitators, participants and managers of participants. We all have a role in making it work. All stakeholders must understand these roles and how they can influence the ultimate outcomes.

7 Be proactive

Anticipate outcomes. Peter Drucker stated so eloquently that, 'It's a manager's job to anticipate the future.' So we have to anticipate the type of data we may need in the future. We cannot assume that our funding stream will always exist. We have to constantly ask ourselves, 'Are we providing enough evidence, data and hard facts that convince the individual who is funding this programme that this is a good investment?' If not, then maybe something needs to change. If you wait for the request, it will be too late. We need to drive evaluation and analytics, not wait for others to push them. ROI and analytics need to be on our agenda, not on the agenda of someone else. We want to be proactive by playing on the offence rather than the defence when it comes to the learning investment.

8 Use the results to make improvements

Programme improvement positions the next programme or project to be more successful than the previous one. In essence, we are optimizing the Return on Investment. By optimizing results, we can influence the allocation of funds in the future. We might make the case that certain projects or programmes need additional funding because they yield a better return on the investment, but without the data, it is difficult to make the argument. For example, in our work at the ROI Institute, we have seen that soft skills programmes, when properly aligned, implemented and supported, can yield very high ROIs – much higher than hard skills programmes. These results enable us to make a compelling argument that soft skills programmes should have a larger allocation of the learning and development budget.

The good news is that this new book is designed to focus on all eight of these areas. It provides helpful advice to make these steps come to life.

Why read this book?

A logical question to ask is, 'Why should I read this book?' Here are six important reasons:

1 The authors provide a fresh perspective with a sound approach, integrating many new ideas and sound advice along the way.

2 The book is well researched and written in an understandable, convincing way. It makes readers want to take action.

3 It is laced with examples and case studies that illustrate and amplify what is being discussed in the book.

4 The book emphasizes the use of technology to assist with evaluation. This helps practitioners manage resources and takes some of the pain out of the evaluation challenge. Technology is critical, particularly if you have a large learning function.

5 The authors bring valuable experience with extensive background in this area. They are not novice beginners, but veterans in this field.

6 The authors are backed by a well-respected organization. CEB is one of the most respected and influential research, benchmarking and consulting organizations.

Call to action

Just reading a book is not what is necessary. As with any knowledge, it has to be put into action. The key is to recognize that change is needed. Wherever you are along the evaluation maturity continuum, there is room for improvement. When it comes to accountability requirements, change is inevitable, but progress is optional.

This book offers several options, approaches and actions that need to be taken at different points. Make plans to implement smart action steps and check your progress. Consider a discussion group with colleagues as you read certain sections or chapters of this book. Re-plan your strategy and adjust as needed. Reach out to the authors for amplification, clarification and additional assistance as necessary.

Just remember, when it comes to showing the value of your programmes, hope is not a strategy, luck is not a factor and doing nothing is not an option. Take the lead and use this book to make it work.

Good luck on your journey.

Jack J Phillips, PhD   Patti P Phillips, PhD
Chairman, ROI Institute   President, ROI Institute

Founders of the ROI Institute and authors of over 75 books on assessment, measurement, evaluation and analytics.

ACKNOWLEDGEMENTS

We would like to thank the following for all their advice during the writing of this book: Jaime Roca, Sari Wilde, Lauren Smith, Justin Taylor, Todd Harrison, Brian Kropp, Kent Barnett, Jeffrey Berk, Kendall Kerekes, Peggy Parskey, Kelly Grant, Rachel Baghelai and Kelly Suh.

Why now? The occasion for learning analytics

An introduction by Jean Martin, Talent Solutions Architect, CEB

By all merits, now is a great time to be managing talent and working in Human Resources. The convergence of three factors – data availability, technology changing the way talent analytics work gets done, and novel insights into employee behaviour – makes the workforce a rich area for further analysis and within bounds to be optimized alongside other business inputs.

Data availability

Without question, organizations are investing in data as a source of information. Leaders understand the value proposition that talent transforms the business and talent leads to competitive advantage. As such, they want a more precise understanding of their talent that has already been hired (and will be hired in the near future). Not surprisingly, CEOs and boards today are focused on the new opportunities talent creates: they know that talent matters. As one example of the link between talent and organizational performance, a study across 203 businesses showed that organizations with strong leadership benches have doubled their profit and revenue growth compared to those with weak benches.[1] Sixty per cent of top-performing companies (as measured against a peer benchmark across a three-year period) report that their boards have a strong understanding of talent issues, as opposed to just 30 per cent of bottom-performing companies. Not surprisingly, given the tie to business results, CEOs want to know more about the talent in their organizations.

PwC's 15th Annual Global CFO Survey showed nearly 100 per cent of CEOs report that the following talent issues are important: staff productivity, employees' views and needs, labour costs, assessments of internal advancement, costs of employee turnover and overall ROI on human capital.[2] However, the average number of CEOs who believe the information they receive in these areas is comprehensive is just 25 per cent. Fundamentally, the data that organizations have today on human capital is not meeting leaders' needs.

Changing the way talent analytics work gets done

HR departments the world over are increasing their HR analytics capabilities. In part this is a reaction to the distrust CEOs maintain regarding the quality and comprehensiveness of HR data. In CEB'S 2013 HR Analytics survey, a full 95 per cent of senior HR leaders said that they would increase investments in HR data and analytics in the following two years.[3] Interestingly, the early results from these investments are disappointing. In 2013, only 15 per cent of senior business leaders agreed with the statement: 'HR analytics has led me to change a business decision in the past year',[4] and only 8 per cent of HR leaders said they believed they are getting significant returns on analytics investments.[5] As one HR vice president in a mining company said, 'There is a lot of data out there but not a lot of information.'[6] Business leaders and HR executives are aligned in asking, 'How can we get more from our HR analytics investments?'

The demand for better, more precise talent analytics is growing and the first place that leaders turn to is the vendors who supply systems for managing talent. Vendors continue to improve the features and benefits of their systems, yet HR leaders are frustrated by four common characteristics of most data-driven HR and talent solutions:

1 Lack of scientific foundation
In many cases, talent management solutions are not proven to drive business outcomes or even improvements in the metrics that the business is looking for.

2 Lack of specificity

Most talent management solutions are generic, off-the-shelf, one-size-fits-all solutions, failing to take into account the context in which the challenge is being felt, whether that be business context, financial context or resource and organizational capability.

3 Lack of actionability

Most talent data is not sufficiently prescriptive as to recommended action steps, providing just data alone with little real insight.

4 Lack of innovation

Many talent management solutions are not innovative; firms and individuals must work extensively to ensure the solutions apply to the modern work life and many of these solutions have been rolled out exactly the same way for hundreds of other organizations and their leaders.

The business models from many talent management providers do not allow them to correct for these inefficiencies. Organizational inertia (eg 'we've always done it this way') seems to be a common driver for lacklustre innovation. Margin requirements and scalable opportunities mean that technical execution is paramount, and because these organizations lack the patience to reinvent, they continue to use HR interventions like stale talent programmes that they have used for decades. Sadly, these old techniques are insufficient to achieve business goals now and will grow more obsolete within the next five years.

The challenge of creating meaningful talent analytics is amplified by the reality that, despite many factors supporting a new potential impact for HR, the modern work environment also poses significant challenges as HR tries to get the job done. Walking the increasingly virtual halls of organizations now, compared to a decade ago, employees and managers feel fundamentally new dynamics around them. The workforce has globalized. Even in small organizations, parts of work – whether internally or externally managed – invariably happen in locations well outside the headquarters' city and often the headquarters' country. The workforce is more diverse than ever: millennials now comprise more than 34 per cent of the workforce and people of diverse backgrounds are critical drivers of success.[7] Multi-generational trends have created urgent needs for changes in strategy and focus across many HR processes. For example, the knowledge transfer from retiring workers is essential to prevent critical information walking out the door. Additionally, multinational corporations are shifting from expat-centric management to local talent investments. The way work happens has changed as well, making management of these new dynamics more difficult. In the new work environment, managers spend significantly less time directly with their teams; spans of control have doubled and most managers manage staff in locations other than where they reside, further reducing manager intimacy with team and individual work.

This new work environment is one in which performance at all levels depends on the ability to capture the value of information and resources outside one's traditional domain. CEB benchmarks revealed that leaders who work as 'Enterprise Leaders', working with and through others, have double the impact on the business than leaders who do not.[8] More and more this is an area where companies are assessing leaders' competencies and driving development. This network-based approach to learning and performance is key to enabling an organization to leverage its collective people assets. These first two changes (workforce diversity and work environment) are deeply affected by talent shortages and emerging skill scarcities especially in areas like STEM and cross-functional roles, creating urgency for HR to evolve its insight into current and future labour markets.

Lastly, HR is challenged by new demands coming from business leaders and managers. Managers are more involved than ever in talent decisions, feeling even more urgency around the criticality of talent to their business outcomes. This means HR is increasingly called upon to provide better data and reporting, especially as other functions have evolved their reporting capability. The traditional HR reports, which offer a retrospective on process and activities without linkages to business metrics and priorities, are seen as woefully outdated. 'Why can't HR analytics look more like sales analytics or operations analytics?' is a constant refrain. As one senior vice president in a large manufacturing company put it: 'When we make our finance decisions, we use data and spreadsheets. When we make decisions about our most important asset, our people, we don't have the same tools.'[9]

Providing unique insight into employee behaviour

HR analytics will continue to gain strategic importance among business leaders. What the business shares with human resources is a vision for improved analytics insights about people. But not just any insights. Business leaders are calling upon HR to move from reporting to analytics; from using data to provide talent reports to using analytics to improve business decisions. The transitions that comprise the shift are covered in Figure 1.1 below.[10]

Figure 1.1 Transitioning from reports to analytics for HR

CEB defines talent analytics as the discovery and communication of meaningful patterns in talent data. Let's unpack a few important terms in this definition:

1 Discovery – key to analytics is the pursuit of new insight or understanding previously unknown. Data collection for the sole purpose of confirming assumptions is not analytics.

2 Communication – just as the tree falling in the forest unheard may not exist, analyses that are not understood by a target audience do not have impact. Communication is critical to seeing analytics take root in driving business outcomes.

3 Meaningful patterns – analytics must produce patterns that are meaningful to the business, addressing important questions upon which action depends.

4 Talent data – as you will see throughout this book, there are many sources of data that will be relevant to understanding the larger talent capabilities in the organization. It will be critical for all leaders to prioritize which data is most important to the business questions at hand and ensure high-quality data in those areas. It is not necessary to have extensive data collection systems in place to do effective analytics – what matters most to effective analytics is the quality not the quantity of data against the question to be answered.

In this context, high-quality data enables talent analytics to be business-led and actionable. As we will discuss further in Chapter 9, CEB's research on talent analytics shows the businesses that value and utilize analytics are characterized not by sophisticated data/information systems, nor by the sophistication in statistical approaches. Rather, analytics that are used and valued are distinguished by: 1) the degree to which the workforce analytics prioritize talent areas most important to the business by engaging with key stakeholders to identify where to apply analytics, and 2) the degree to which the workforce analytics utilize a variety of techniques that inform business decisions and provide actionable guidance. In short, business alignment and actionable guidance trump sophistication when it comes to driving value through talent analytics.

Yet, to attain these hallmarks of successful analytics, most organizations face a steep climb. Only 17 per cent of business leaders surveyed report that they believe HR analytics focuses on the right business outcomes and only 18 per cent trust the data they receive from HR.[11] HR needs a way to close the gap on the 3Cs:

- criticality of the metrics measured;
- capability of HR staff doing and delivering the analysis;
- credibility of HR data as a business-driving tool.

Chapter 9 digs deeper into this issue and provides case study examples. Business leaders are voting with their feet. That is, they are walking away from the tools available to them that can help make informed decisions. Fewer than 25 per cent of business leaders surveyed said they use HR data to source talent, improve employee performance, select high-potentials, design the organization or manage succession.[12] As many in HR pursue additional resources to support evolving talent priorities, the function struggles to demonstrate its relevance and ongoing impact on the business.

The learning analytics opportunity

Perhaps the HR domain in which the challenge to demonstrate impact is clearest is the learning function where learning and development (L&D) leaders are feeling the heat from stakeholders. Sixty-four per cent of CEOs cite building a skilled workforce as a top priority, and 77 per cent of heads of L&D report an increase in demands from the business to demonstrate business impact.[13] As you might expect, the current report card on the learning function is not encouraging. Only 33 per cent of business leaders think that the L&D function impacts business outcomes, and fewer consider the function to be relevant or timely.[14] On the positive side, business leaders do feel compelled to take ownership: 67 per cent of business leaders report they are held more accountable for providing talent development opportunities to their teams.[15]

Organizations of all types are reporting that learning itself has evolved in both how much is learned and how it is learned. With the changing work environment and the constant availability of information and knowledge at their fingertips, employees are seeking information much more frequently and through many more channels. As you see in Figure 1.2, these new approaches are changing employees' expectations for learning.[16]

Figure 1.2 Key trends driving changes in expectations

57%
of employees expect learning to be more 'just in time' than three years ago.

Only 37%
of employees expect the organization to actively drive their development.

Only 21%
of employees expect most of their learning to happen in a classroom.

A 2014 benchmark revealed employees spending an average of 39 per cent of their time in any given month learning.[17] Unfortunately, learning is not always productive. When performance gains are mapped against the amount of time spent learning, employees are shown to be learning past the point of performance improvement, with potentially 11 per cent of employee time wasted on learning that does not result in better performance. That lost time comes at a cost of millions of dollars.[18]

Figure 1.3   Percentage of employee work time spent learning skills and processing information

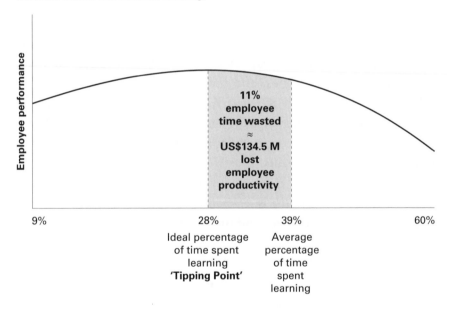

Time spent learning new skills or processing new information related to job tasks (includes formal and informal learning)

11% employee time wasted ≈ US$134.5 M lost employee productivity

9%   28%   39%   60%

Ideal percentage of time spent learning **'Tipping Point'**

Average percentage of time spent learning

It is not unusual for the largest companies to provide thousands of development programmes across their workforce. Even small organizations can be saturated by internal and external development opportunities. CEB's Unified Benchmarking platform indicates that overall learning activity in the organization has increased: 64 per cent more organizations are participating in more formal learning than two years ago,[19] and the percentage of employees actively learning from peers rose from 51 per cent to 69 per cent from 2012 to 2014.[20,21]

But what are these activities really worth in terms of their benefit to the bottom-line results?

As one would expect, results are mixed. Some talent development programmes have outsized impact and others have little to no impact. What is even more concerning than the variable levels of impact is the fact that most companies have no way to track and report whether these opportunities influence business outcomes. Commonly reported metrics on talent development programmes are 'the degree to which instructor met the expectations for the course' and 'participant satisfaction', both of which are collected immediately after training. Only rarely do organizations determine whether the development programmes accomplished the desired changes in behaviour and capabilities. Worse yet, the application of desired behaviours and capabilities on the job is evaluated even less often. As we will discuss later in this book, CEB benchmarks show that on average, 45 per cent of the programme content is not applied back on the job.[22] If 45 per cent of training is wasted as 'scrap learning', the cost of development immediately goes up. Scrap learning is rightly keeping CFOs up at night.

What explains this wasted learning? Data is revealing here. Learning is often redundant and, even worse, low quality. On average, only 32 per cent of the spend by the L&D function was considered high quality and not redundant in 2014.[23] See Figure 1.4.

To understand this better, picture an average employee. This employee may be mid-career and facing a wide variety of skill-building options from external executive education programmes offered by their manager to free online resources. If this employee's experience maps to the data above, one-third of what he or she receives will be low quality. Plus, the content within these separate learning experiences is also likely to overlap, providing redundant and wasted learning. Similarly, learning done outside the formal L&D function is nearly as bad, with 25 per cent of the spend going unapplied and another 20 per cent being redundant.

To avoid these costs, learning analytics must also evolve, just as learning has evolved. In this book, we will seek to guide you and your organization through some recent evolutions. In Chapter 1, we have explored research about how learning is changing within organizations.

Figure 1.4   Wasted learning inside and outside the L&D function

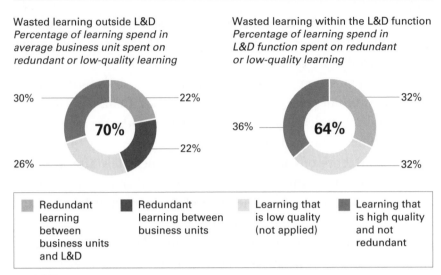

Wasted learning outside L&D
*Percentage of learning spend in
average business unit spent on
redundant or low-quality learning*

Wasted learning within the L&D function
*Percentage of learning spend in
L&D function spent on redundant
or low-quality learning*

| | Redundant learning between business units and L&D | | Redundant learning between business units | | Learning that is low quality (not applied) | | Learning that is high quality and not redundant |

n = 1,519.

SOURCE: CEB 2015 L&D Functional Effectiveness Survey
NOTE: Totals may not equal 100 per cent due to rounding

In Chapter 2 we define learning analytics, and share what makes it valuable to the business. Chapter 3 explores the role of technology in the evaluation process – how it makes learning analytics more efficient and effective. Chapter 4 focuses on business impact, in particular, what methods should be used to quantify the influence of development programmes on business measures? Chapter 5 raises the issue of scrap learning, how to measure it and why it should be used as a leading indicator of success. Chapter 6 addresses the fact that learning analytics begins at the beginning, not the end of development programmes. That is, successful talent development programmes start with effective needs analysis and learning analytics is an integral part. Chapter 7 highlights the usefulness of benchmarks and where they can be found. In Chapter 8 we focus on using analytics to optimize the impact of programmes on the business by monitoring efficiency and effectiveness measures. Chapter 9 provides a broader perspective beyond learning analytics by examining how technology and analytics will inform talent leaders in the near future.

It is an exciting time to be in HR, particularly as at last we can begin to measure and manage HR's impact on the business with precision, understanding the inputs and expected outputs and the relative ROI of talent interventions. As you will see in the case examples throughout the book, when analytics provide leaders with the type of business-oriented and actionable insight they are looking for, human resources supports the business and drives it forward in important and dramatic ways – if only we take the time to measure and improve our impact. Learning analytics is driving the improvement of talent development programmes and business results. The rest of this book explains why and how.

Endnotes

1 CEB analysis (2016) Managing the Board of Directors, internal CEB report.

2 PwC (2012) 15th Annual Global CEO Survey [online] https://www.pwc.com/gx/en/ceo-survey/pdf/15th-global-pwc-ceo-survey.pdf.

3 5 8 CEB (2013) Corporate Leadership Council Analytics Survey, internal CEB report.

4 CEB (2013) Business Barometer [online] https://www.cebglobal.com/blogs/files/2013/08/FLC6674913SYN-BRF-Bus-Barometer-Q3-Agg-Findings.pdf.

6 10 23 CEB (2013) The Analytics Era: Transforming HR's impact on the business [online] https:www.cebglobal.com/shl/images/uploads/linkau13-CLC-The-Analytics-Era.pdf.

7 Richard Fry (11 May 2015) Millennials Surpass Gen Xers as the Largest Generation in US Labor Force, Pew Research Center [online] http://www.pewresearch.org/fact-tank/2015/05/11/millennials-surpass-gen-xers-as-the-largest-generation-in-u-s-labor-force/.

9 11 12 CEB (2013) Global Labor Market Survey, internal CEB report.

13 PwC (2014) 17th Annual Global CEO Survey [online] http://www.pwc.com/gx/en/sustainability/ceo-views/assets/pwc-ceo-summary-sustainability.pdf.

14 15 23 CEB (2015) L&D Functional Effectiveness Survey, internal CEB report.

16 17 18 19 21 CEB (2014) Learning Culture Survey, internal CEB report.

20 CEB (2012) New Work Environment Study, internal CEB report.

22 CEB (2015) Scrap Learning Research, CEB marketing materials.

Access to the CEB resources cited in this book is limited to members. For information about membership, please contact CEB's Member Support Centre at CEB.Support@cebglobal.com or +1-866-913-2632.

What is learning analytics? 02

Introduction

There are two distinct worlds of learning analytics. The first focuses on educational systems that prepare young people to join the working world. The research literature is rife with information in this area because K-12 and higher education programmes are measured extensively. Critical success measures include the following: attendance/truancy, curriculum delivery, curriculum variations, normed performance on reading and math skills, special needs at the extremely high and low ends of the learning spectrum, graduation rates, instructor quality, school accreditation and many other measurable aspects of performance for the students, faculty, administration, school and school system.

The second focuses on corporate training and how it prepares learners for their roles and responsibilities within an organization. This book focuses exclusively on this second area – evaluation within organizational learning and development groups (often called corporate universities) that develop talent internally to meet organizational needs. This also includes corporate organizations that provide training to external learners, such as customers who purchase software products and need training in order to successfully implement and use them. Throughout this text, we will refer to these two groups as corporate universities and learning providers.

There are many definitions of learning analytics. Our preferred definition is the following:

> Learning analytics is the science and art of gathering, processing, interpreting and reporting data related to the efficiency, effectiveness and business impact of development programmes designed to improve individual and organizational performance and inform stakeholders.

The primary focus of learning analytics is to determine whether a learning experience is effective or not. The way effectiveness is defined and measured varies. In its simplest form, effectiveness might relate to knowledge and skills gained during training. A more complex measure might be the impact of training on a business metric such as sales growth or revenue. Because training is not a liberal arts education – that is, training is designed to improve on-the-job performance and business performance by transferring usable knowledge and skills – we highly recommend measuring for impact on business metrics, not just transfer of knowledge. A wide variety of effectiveness measures will be discussed in this and later chapters.

Learning analytics also provides data for continuous improvement. Results help determine what needs to change, such as the course materials, instructors, the environment, learning methodologies, etc – anything that can be enhanced to improve the overall quality of the learning experience.

It is worth examining a few key words and phrases in our definition of learning analytics:

- Science guides the way data is collected using valid and reliable collection instruments, such as surveys, knowledge and skills tests, interviews, on-the-job performance checklists and similar tools.

- Likewise, the best practices from technology companies are applied for storing extremely large data sets in relational tables with tags so the data can be categorized logically and rapidly retrieved for analysis and reporting. Scientific rigour is applied when processing data using descriptive, predictive and prescriptive statistical approaches to unlock patterns in the data set.

- Results are interpreted for statistical and practical significance, often by comparing them to benchmarks and historical trends.

- A variety of data visualization practices are applied to transform data into insights. While scientific rigour is the foundation to the learning analytics process, art is also essential for effective communication to stakeholders.

- A final word in the definition of learning analytics is worth considering: organization. It is meant to convey a wide variety of organizations such as for-profit, non-profit and not-for-profit businesses. Our definition intends to encompass all organizations and their multiple and varied indicators of success for individuals and the organization. For example, for-profit businesses provide sales training to increase sales and drive revenue. Even government organizations that are aligned to non-financial goals can use this definition simply by substituting 'mission impact' for 'business impact'. We focus on applying learning analytics to organizations that want to demonstrate individual and organizational improvement as a result of development programmes.

Now that we have a full explanation of our definition of learning analytics, let's examine how measurement practices in the talent development space have evolved.

Learning analytics today: measure for measure, what should be measured?

Leaders of learning organizations often struggle with what *should* be measured. The options seem endless. In the end, many organizations report what is available, such as the number of people trained, the cost per learning hour and the type of learning methodology used to deliver training. Other organizations focus on measures of effectiveness such as the amount of knowledge gained during training or the intent to apply skills back on the job. Still others focus on measures that align to business needs such as decreasing cycle time, increasing customer satisfaction or driving revenue.

CEB's 2014 poll of leaders of learning organizations revealed that the majority (77 per cent) of L&D executives consider learning measurement a priority for their organization. L&D functions are measuring more learning activity and using more metrics than ever before.[1] Figure 2.1 shows the types of measures learning leaders gather to determine impact.

Results show that the majority of organizations collect learning satisfaction data and use it to assess learning impact. Slightly more than half also made notable progress in capturing and using data on learning application. However, fewer than one-third measure the

Figure 2.1 Measures used by learning leaders to assess impact

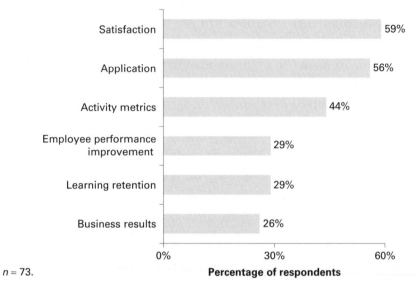

Beyond satisfaction in learning data
Percentage of L&D executives identifying metrics used to assess learning impact

Satisfaction 59%
Application 56%
Activity metrics 44%
Employee performance improvement 29%
Learning retention 29%
Business results 26%

n = 73.   **Percentage of respondents**

SOURCE: CEB L&D Leadership Council: Quick Poll Results (2014)

impact of learning on employee performance and business results. It is important to note that satisfaction is the most frequently gathered measure, but it is also the least valuable measure with regards to impact. Later in this chapter, we'll explore the reasons why organizations measure satisfaction rather than impact, but first, let's understand the business case for learning analytics.

Why measure learning?

In 2010, KnowledgeAdvisors, now part of CEB, surveyed learning leaders and found that measurement was deployed for two main reasons: first, to determine the effectiveness of training (impact) and second, to gather information to identify gaps for continuous improvement.[2] Figure 2.2 shows the full set of responses to the question, 'Why do you deploy measurement within your corporate university?'

Figure 2.2 Common reasons measurement is used

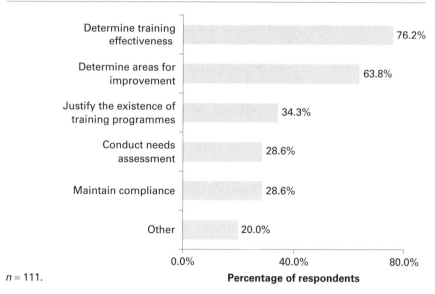

n = 111.

SOURCE: KnowledgeAdvisors (2010)

Recognizing that talent development comes at a significant cost, learning organizations are using measures to understand its effectiveness, to decide what needs to change or be added and to build the business case for development programmes to continue. The need for these business cases has been heightened as CEOs have turned their attention to returns on human capital investments. PwC's study of CEOs' opinions on the ROI of human capital investments reveals that most CEOs feel they lack comprehensive information about talent-related investments.[3] CEOs and CFOs want to know, 'Where should we spend our organization's money to achieve business results?' and 'Where will I get the biggest bang for my buck?' These are effectiveness questions that are often difficult to answer, but it is essential to provide answers to them because development groups that cannot do so are often the first to have their budgets cut in lean economic times.

CEB's 2013 benchmark of boards of directors also showed board members asking for more talent-related information in order to understand and manage business risks.[4] Because training budgets are a major talent-related cost, boards and CEOs want significantly more insight into the value of the training their employees are receiving. The C-suites and boards are creating a demand for information that most development groups cannot supply.

Beyond the need for information about the impact of learning programmes, there is a more pressing need for learning analytics. Talent is often the largest overhead cost for an organization (eg payroll), and anything that makes that cost more effective will add value to the business. Not only is payroll a cost, but curricula represent an ongoing investment as well. In exchange for these costs, learning organizations attempt to drive productivity that adds value directly to the bottom line. Yet, without measurement, business leaders are left only with intuition and anecdotal information about training's influence. In the end, the development function is seen as a cost centre rather than a business partner that can demonstrate value.

Organizations that measure effectiveness can show how their programmes influence business outcomes. They connect training to a variety of critical business measures, including retention/turnover, new employee referrals, internal promotions, quality, production, customer service, innovation, revenue, sales, market share, safety, product development and employee engagement. When learning organizations demonstrate their value, business leaders are able to decide how to leverage this powerful business influencer to accomplish strategic goals. The lynchpin for demonstrating this value is learning analytics.

Most organizations start with the simple: measure training adoption and satisfaction

When evaluating training, adoption measures are easy to gather, such as the number of courses in the curriculum and the number of people who have attended training. Costs associated with each course are often easy to produce as well. When combined, they can provide insight about adoption of learning products such as the cost per course, cost per learning methodology or even the re-use ratio of e-learning products. These measures provide direct value, especially when managing vendors that supply learning products. For example, when managing a vendor that provides e-learning content, the adoption rate (number of courses consumed divided by the number of potential consumers (eg employees)) provides good insight into how much of the e-learning content is needed. This measure can help a product manager buy only a portion of the curriculum rather than an entire library and thus save the organization some money. The Association for Talent Development (ATD) publishes the *State of the Industry Report* annually, which provides benchmarks by industry and training type for a variety of adoption measures.[5]

But most organizations want more than just participation rates; they also want to measure quality. And who better to judge that than the participant? Most organizations have implemented 'smile sheets' or post-training surveys to hear from the participant how they felt the training went. Measuring the satisfaction of learners with their training offers useful input into how learners experienced the training. Did they like the instructor? Did they understand the material? But sadly, measuring learners' satisfaction with the training experience does very little to measure whether they will actually apply what they have learned.

In fact, both adoption and satisfaction measures have limited value in demonstrating the impact of a learning experience, leaving learning leaders to scratch their heads, wondering, 'How can I show the effectiveness of the courses that are deployed rather than just how many people were trained and liked the training?' More importantly, the learning leaders often receive pressure from business leaders to provide measures beyond adoption and satisfaction. The CEO wants to know if the training works. Are the programmes that are designed to improve critical competencies actually developing appropriate knowledge, skills and abilities among learners? Adoption and satisfaction measures do not answer these questions.

Furthermore, the CFO wants to know if training programmes are a good investment for the organization. She and the CHRO must decide whether it is more cost effective to build or buy talent. Should the organization spend more money on developing resources in-house through training (build) or should it hire highly qualified and capable individuals who require little development (buy). A combination of efficiency, effectiveness and business outcome measures is required to answer her questions.

Efficiency, effectiveness and business outcomes: closing the learning measurement gap

In 2010 Jack and Patti Phillips of the ROI Institute published an article in *Chief Learning Officer* magazine that captured the information needs of CEOs with regards to training.[6] They asked executives about the value of what currently gets measured and what should be measured when it comes to managing training. The results were presented in a tabular format in the magazine. CEB has reformatted the results in graphic form in Figure 2.3 to emphasize the large gap between what is currently measured and what should be measured.

Figure 2.3 What CEOs want learning leaders to measure

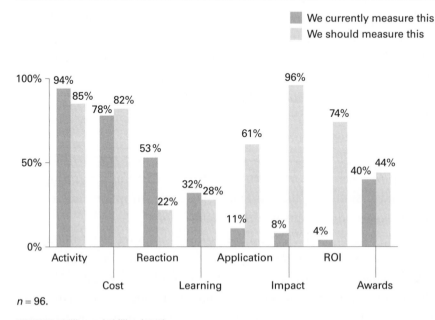

n = 96.

SOURCE: Phillips and Phillips (2010)

The results are clear and compelling. Most organizations have focused on measuring activity and cost on the left side of the graph. Leaders want this information, and L&D appears to be meeting that need. However, very few leaders, roughly 20 per cent, want to know about Reaction (aka Satisfaction) or Learning (25 per cent). In contrast, more than 60 per cent want to know about Application, Impact and ROI, and nearly 100 per cent are focused on Impact. The great disconnect here is that very few organizations, fewer than 10 per cent, measure it. The disparity between these 'current' vs 'should' measures is extreme.

The message from this research is clear: it is a manifesto for talent development leaders who want to address the information needs of their business leaders. They should monitor activity and cost, but also provide evaluative information about the impact and value of training. The information they supply should answer the questions, 'Will training be applied? Will it improve individual and organizational performance? Will the investment in training pay off in terms of real business benefits?' Fortunately, learning measurement approaches have evolved to help answer these questions.

The journey to learning analytics

Learning analytics has grown from a vast body of research, much of it derived from evaluative efforts to determine the best way to educate children in schools. Its roots are grounded in statistical techniques, methodological designs and programme evaluation, which is defined as:

> a systematic method for collecting, analysing and using information to answer questions about projects, policies and programmes, particularly about their effectiveness and efficiency.[7]

A programme can be a health-based protocol to quit smoking or a class about presentation skills. The explicit purpose of the *evaluation* is to measure the inputs and activities of a programme, a process called formative evaluation, and then track the outcomes of the programme, a process called summative evaluation.[8] Two leading texts that establish the foundations of programme evaluation as a field of study include *Evaluation: A systematic approach*[8] and *Foundations of Program Evaluation: Theories of practice.*[9]

Like any area of study, there are many theories and approaches, but a few rise to the top because they are the most comprehensive, the most parsimonious, or the most practical. In the field of instructional design, there are only a handful of frequently used approaches for creating effective training programmes, such as Merrill's First Principles of Instruction[10] and Gagné's Nine Events of Instructional Design.[11] The most commonly used approach is the ADDIE model.[12] The five steps in the model are simple and intuitive: Analysis, Design, Develop, Implement and Evaluate.

Learning analytics plays a critical role in the ADDIE model at the beginning and end. During the Analysis phase, instructional designers conduct a needs assessment to gather information about the knowledge and skills gaps of their audience and critical tasks are aligned to successful performance. These efforts are essential for creating a course that is aligned to the business needs of the organization and fills performance gaps for the workforce. After training has been implemented, instructional designers begin the Evaluate phase, gathering data to determine if participants learned new knowledge and skills and can successfully apply them on the job.

The ADDIE model is a linear process in its design, but it is cyclical in practice when a course is deployed several times. Information gathered during the Evaluate phase at the end of one programme can be used to inform the Analysis phase for the next deployment. The Assessment, Measurement and Evaluation group at JetBlue Airways emphasizes this perspective:

> As faculty became more motivated to conduct impact evaluations, they became more aware of the need to have clearly defined goals at the beginning of the project. Needs assessment and evaluation are essentially two sides of the same coin.[13]

See the JetBlue case study later in this chapter for more details.

Among the many evaluation approaches available, only a few are widely used. These include Kirkpatrick's Four Levels of Evaluation,[14]

Phillips' ROI Methodology,[15] Bersin's Impact Measurement Framework,[16] Brinkerhoff's Success Case Method,[17] and Hale's performance-based evaluation approach.[18] All of these methods are described here because they have contributed substantially to the advancement of training evaluation and learning analytics.

The Four Levels of Evaluation

The history of corporate training evaluation as we know it today began in the late 1950s with Donald Kirkpatrick and his dissertation. While consulting with a client, he developed a simple approach to evaluate the impact of training on performance consisting of four levels: Reaction, Learning, Behaviour and Results. The levels align with a specific set of questions.

- **Level 1 Reaction** – focuses on learners' reactions to training. Are they satisfied with training? Was the course valuable? Was the instructor capable? Were objectives met? Did the facilities support the delivery of the course?

- **Level 2 Learning** – focuses on the acquisition of knowledge and skills during training. Did attendees learn new information and skills?

- **Level 3 Behaviour** – addresses the impact of learning on individual performance. Are learners able to apply training back on the job? If so, to what extent does it improve individual performance?

- **Level 4 Results** – focuses on results for the business. Does training help improve critical business metrics such as employee morale, customer satisfaction, sales, productivity, revenue, etc?

In 1956, Donald Kirkpatrick published an article titled 'How to Start an Objective Evaluation of Your Training Program',[19] in the May–June issue of *The Journal of the American Society of Training Directors* – the predecessor to *T+D Magazine*. He gave simple yet sage advice about how to determine the effectiveness of training. Thus, the first version of the Four Levels of Evaluation was brought to the public spotlight. Later books such as *Evaluating Training*

Programs: The four levels,[20] *Transferring Learning to Behaviors,*[21] and *Implementing the Four Levels*[22] provided a much more detailed evaluation methodology to support the four levels.

For more than 50 years Kirkpatrick applied his model with clients and actively taught others how to use it. His son, Jim Kirkpatrick, and daughter-in-law, Wendy Kirkpatrick, carry on his legacy through their company Kirkpatrick Partners. Recently, Kirkpatrick Partners refreshed the four levels, bringing a more modern approach and comprehensive methodology to evaluation. Figure 2.4 shows that the Four Levels of Evaluation are used most often among various evaluation approaches.[23]

Figure 2.4 Most frequently used models for evaluating talent development

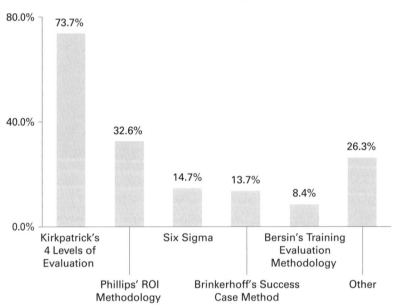

n = 111.

SOURCE: KnowledgeAdvisors (2010)

The Return on Investment training methodology

The Return on Investment (ROI) Methodology used to evaluate talent development programmes was developed by Jack Phillips based on his research and consulting work in the early 1980s. He and his wife Patti, the president and CEO of the ROI Institute, continue to deploy and refine the approach, which is often referred to as the five levels of evaluation for good reason. The first four levels are similar in name and function to Kirkpatrick's four levels. They are: Reaction and Planned Action, Learning, Application and Impact. Phillips extends the model to Level 5 with a focus on Return on Investment.[24] The emphasis on ROI comes from Phillips' experience with business leaders who were interested in the impact of training but often misunderstood the language used by learning and development professionals. ROI alleviates much of the miscommunication because business leaders understand the simple formula for ROI (ROI = (Benefits – Costs) / Costs) and how it is used in other areas of the business. As mentioned earlier, leaders are also interested in impact, and ROI provides a monetized assessment of training's impact in one simple measure.

It is important to note that the five levels are only one part of the ROI Methodology, which is a systematic approach that incorporates evaluation planning, data collection, data analysis and reporting. The process, not just the five levels, is the heart of the ROI Methodology. Additionally, the methodology can be applied to other HR interventions, not just training programmes.

It is also worth noting that the ROI Methodology includes Level 0. Phillips added this level as a way of incorporating measures of training activity such as the total number of people trained, the learning methodology used for training and the cost of training.

During an ROI conference in Amsterdam in 2004, Diederick Stoel interviewed Don Kirkpatrick and Jack Phillips on stage, letting these heavyweight thought leaders spar.[25] Both men acknowledged the similarities in their models. Phillips admitted to using Kirkpatrick's model with his clients and those efforts eventually led to the ROI

Methodology. Kirkpatrick acknowledged that ROI should be a separate level, and they discussed Phillips' relabelling of Level 3 from Application to Behaviour and Level 4 from Results to Business Impact. Notably, both families have advised and influenced the development of CEB's Metrics That Matter™ product during its early years. Together, these men and their families laid the foundation for evaluation of talent development programmes as we know them today.

Impact Measurement Framework

In 2007, Josh Bersin added a new perspective to the evaluation debate when he published *The Training Measurement Book*.[26] He felt the Kirkpatrick and Phillips models missed an important aspect of the process – the beginning – where measurement determines whether the learning solution is aligned to the needs of the business.

Rather than just four levels, or a fifth level for ROI, Bersin outlined nine critical measures which form the basis for his Impact Measurement Framework:

- **Satisfaction** – captures the direct feedback from learners about various aspects of training (eg Kirkpatrick's Level 1 Reaction).

- **Learning** – reflects whether training attendees gained knowledge and skill (eg Kirkpatrick's Level 2 Learning). Bersin focuses on the extent to which training objectives were achieved.

- **Adoption** – refers to the percentage of the target population that has completed a given programme; this is more than just the standard 'butts in seats' measure because it incorporates the target population, implying that not every employee should attend.

- **Utility** – reflects the usefulness of the course for individual learners and work groups. Bersin claims that this measure is a surrogate of performance and serves as an easy-to-gather (compared to actual performance measurement) leading indicator of performance.

- **Efficiency** – is a measure of learning activities divided by costs. Like Adoption, Efficiency measures are not based on the opinions of learners. Rather, they are based on factual activity and cost figures. Efficiency measures include: cost/hour of content development, cost/hour of delivery, cost/learner and cost/learning hour by delivery type (eg e-learning, ILT, VILT, etc).

- **Alignment** – refers to the continuous process of making sure training programmes address the most urgent and critical business problems for the organization; a standard needs assessment helps an organization create job alignment and competency alignment. Bersin suggests measuring training alignment to the following aspects of business: investment, process, management, financial, urgency and time.

- **Attainment of client objectives** – reflects the need to measure customer satisfaction with training programmes. How satisfied are stakeholders with training's ability to meet business needs?

- **Individual performance** – refers to the on-the-job performance of training attendees (eg Kirkpatrick's Level 3).

- **Organizational performance** – focuses on the ability to demonstrate the link between training, individual performance and improved performance on business metrics. Suggested metrics include: employee engagement, employee retention, flexibility and mobility in the workforce, hiring rates, employment brand – any measure that is determined mission-critical for the business (eg Kirkpatrick's Level 4).

Compared to the models proposed by Kirkpatrick and Phillips, Bersin's model is more comprehensive in that it consolidates measures of efficiency (adoption and efficiency), effectiveness (satisfaction, utility and alignment) and business outcomes (client objectives, individual performance and organizational performance). Among these, utility and alignment are the concepts that stand apart from predecessors.

Success Case Method

The Success Case Method[27] (SCM) is a dramatically different approach to training evaluation compared to the previous models, offering a methodology with a faster time course and a stronger reliance on qualitative information.

Robert Brinkerhoff, a retired researcher with a successful career as a professor at Western Michigan University, developed the Success Case Method when considering the impact of training on business metrics. He argued that existing training evaluation models tended to be myopic, focusing too much of the investigation on training as a driver of performance and too little on the other factors that might influence it.

Brinkerhoff writes that SCM 'combines the ancient craft of story-telling with more current evaluation approaches of naturalistic inquiry and case study'.[28] The heart of the methodology revolves around two audiences – those who are successful and those who are not. The goal is to determine the drivers of success and failure for both groups.

The methodology for SCM is relatively simple and for this reason many evaluators prefer it because it can be implemented quickly to gather critical information. The first step is to gather a sample of quantitative data from participants. When conducting an evaluation of a learning programme, this usually entails distributing a survey to learners immediately after training. The survey should be brief, roughly five questions long, and it should focus on the key aspects of the programme that are believed to contribute to successful performance.

A unique aspect of the SCM is the way data is analysed. Rather than focusing on the average scores on the survey questions, SCM focuses on the extreme scores – the high and low ends of the response distribution. The purpose is to identify the people who will be (or have been) successful when applying knowledge and skills on the job as well as those who will not be (or have not been) successful.

The second step in the methodology is to gather much more detailed information from the successful and non-successful groups through key person interviews. Focus groups can also be used. These inquiry approaches allow the evaluator to gather very specific information about performance drivers related to training and other factors beyond training. Results from the SCM are mostly qualitative and tend to provide a rich description of individual and organizational performance. For some evaluators, it is easier to assess cause and effect, impact and areas for improvement using qualitative information than it is to use quantitative data. Qualitative information also tends to be more compelling than quantitative. Compare the following two statements: 'Because of the game-based simulation, I was able to practise my skills over and over, giving me great confidence when I made my first sales call', vs 'The learners were satisfied with training (4.57 vs benchmark of 4.03) and intend to apply what they learned on the job (4.44 vs benchmark of 4.01).'

The complete methodology is described in Brinkerhoff's book, *The Success Case Method.*[29] It includes guidance for developing a logic model before collecting any information and being willing to explore unanticipated drivers of performance. Evaluators find the SCM easy to communicate to stakeholders and easy to apply. The results are valid and reliable and provide logical stories of cause and effect that resonate with stakeholders who are interested in meaningful, easy-to-understand results they can share.

Performance-based evaluation

Judy Hale is a fellow of the International Board of Standards for Training, Performance and Instruction (IBSTPI) and a past president of the International Society for Performance Improvement (ISPI). Her publications focus on helping human resources professionals improve their ability to measure the impact of training on performance and how to create certification programmes.

Two of her books provide sound guidance for conducting training and performance evaluation: *Performance-based Evaluation: Tools and techniques to measure the impact of training*[30] and *Performance-based Certification: How to build a valid, defensible, cost-effective program.*[31]

In her evaluation text, Hale addresses the need to measure both efficiency and effectiveness. This two-part approach is more parsimonious than other models shared here and places a stronger emphasis on efficiency. This is an important distinction because it reflects one of the core tenets of programme evaluation – monitor the way a programme is being implemented and then assess impact (eg formative evaluation and summative evaluation). Monitoring ensures that the programme is deployed as intended. If it is not, the variations are tracked and considered as influencers of programme outcomes. It is a simple yet essential component. Often evaluators assume that a programme is executed as designed and do not monitor it. This is as dangerous as assuming a patient can self-medicate multiple times a day at the prescribed time with the right dosage. Not every patient can. Similarly, not every instructor can deliver course materials as designed. Not every development environment is the same, and every audience differs somewhat due to variations in demographics. Monitoring is essential.

In her text, Hale provides a rationale for measuring both efficiency and effectiveness, and then proceeds to provide practical recommendations for executing a measurement plan. Then she attacks some sacred cows in the training industry – the assumption that certain types of training cannot, or should not, be measured such as soft skills courses, mandated programmes, elective training and employee relations programmes. Without measurement, it is impossible to know how efficient or effective any of these programmes are. Hale's message is clear: measure and find out. The latter portion of her book provides explicit methodological guidance about sampling, data collection and analysis of quantitative and qualitative data.

Hale has also influenced the training evaluation community by defining a clear and rigorous process for developing certification programmes. A critical component of the process is developing criteria for determining quality performance. The criteria are most often assessed by developing and deploying knowledge and skills tests, but criteria can also be gathered from on-the-job experience, work records, endorsements and external credentials.

With regards to testing as an approach to gathering performance evidence, Hale advocates using a criterion-based approach. If a learner can demonstrate competence on a test that correlates with performance, then the learner is likely to perform well on the job. The passing score is based on criteria that align with effective on-the-job performance. The criterion-based testing approach is substantially different from normative-based testing, which is the basis for most large-scale entrance exams such as the SAT, ACT, GMAT, MCAT and others. Scores on these tests reflect a person's performance relative to all other test takers. The top scorer on the test may be smarter than all others, but may not be able to perform to the specific set of criteria required for successful performance on the job. A norm-based test is designed to rank in order the performance of all test takers. A criterion-based test is designed to determine which test takers are competent to perform on the job and which are not.

When building tests, it is essential to focus on performance-based criteria, not simply knowledge acquisition, in order to create an instrument that predicts on-the-job performance. Building a valid and reliable test is not easy and many books provide a how-to approach for test development, including Shrock and Coscarelli,[32] and Osterlind.[33] Hale provides sound guidance for developing criterion-based tests and also couches testing (and other criterion-based evidence-gathering techniques such as experience, work records, endorsements, etc) within a process that flows from the inception of the certification programme to the granting of the certificate.

For Hale, performance improvement can be measured by focusing on a set of performance criteria. To her, those criteria are far more important than satisfaction, learning, intent to apply and other measures from evaluation models. While the approach is much more difficult – it takes more time and effort to define performance criteria and gather performance-based evidence – some evaluators use it because it is a stronger methodology, which aligns training efforts directly with performance on the job.

The models that have been examined so far are summarized in Table 2.1 using the basic structure of Kirkpatrick's Four Levels of Evaluation. Models from Kirkpatrick, Phillips and Bersin fit this structure well, whereas Brinkerhoff and Hale do not.

Table 2.1 Comparison of training evaluations models

Type of measure	Kirkpatrick	Phillips	Bersin	Brinkerhoff	Hale
Level 0		Inputs	Adoption and efficiency	Any or all of these measures can be used to gather quantitative information via a survey; thereafter conduct interviews among those with the highest and lowest ratings	Efficiency
Level 1	Reaction	Reaction and planned action	Satisfaction		Effectiveness
Level 2	Learning	Learning	Learning		Effectiveness
Level 3	Behaviour	Application	Individual performance		Effectiveness – What are the performance criteria?
Level 4	Results	Impact	Organizational performance		Effectiveness – How do criteria link to organizational performance?
Level 5		ROI			Effectiveness
Others		Intangibles	Utility, alignment and attainment of client objectives		Determine criteria for successful performance on the job

CASE STUDY JetBlue University evaluation strategy, certification programme and prediction project

In February 1999 David Neeleman announced the formation of an airline called 'New Air'. Within a year, the company secured an unprecedented set of 75 take-off and landing slots at John F Kennedy airport near New York City, placed a $4 billion order for 75 new A320 Airbus Industries aircraft, and secured a certificate of Public Convenience and Necessity, representing the successful completion of the airline's application processes with both the DOT and the Federal Aviation Administration. It also announced that all seats would be leather and would have access to 24 channels of satellite television in flight. The goal: provide the best coach-class experience in the industry. The name changed to JetBlue Airways and by the end of 2000, the business had registered its one millionth customer and received flown revenue of $100 million. This propitious start launched an airline known for quality, customer service and innovation. It is the only airline to launch in the United States since 1999 that has reached a 15th anniversary.[34]

Evaluation strategy

A culture of innovation spread throughout the organization, including JetBlue University (JBU), which boldly committed itself to excellence by measuring and monitoring its own performance. The Assessment, Measurement and Evaluation (AME) group was formed in 2004 with the express purpose of evaluating the efficiency and effectiveness of JBU's training programmes. Guided by Hale's performance-based evaluation principles, Kirkpatrick's Four Levels of Evaluation and the 10 Standards for Performance Technology from the International Society for Performance Improvement (ISPI),[35] the AME group created a five-phased measurement strategy for the corporate university.[36] The strategy included:

- **Evaluation type** – focused on measuring satisfaction (Level 1), learning (Level 2) and impact (Level 3 and higher).

- **Process for evaluation** – a deliberate approach that provides decision-making support about the extent to which resources should be invested in evaluating each learning programme.

- **Tools to support evaluation** – includes job aids, workshops and technology systems used to execute the evaluation process.

- **Involvement** – ensures ongoing communication with and engagement of stakeholders about the process of evaluation, the results of evaluation efforts and how those results should be interpreted and used.

- **Focus of evaluation** – educates JBU faculty on the purpose of each phase of evaluation, using practical questions so that they can align their data collection needs with the appropriate phase.

In 2009, the AME group published an article which included three detailed case studies about their evaluation efforts, showing that success breeds success.

As operational counterparts were exposed to the clearly defined data collection goals, tools, and targeted results communication, their buy-in for needs assessment and evaluation activities has increased, which paves the way for future data collection efforts. (p 14)[37]

Certification programme

Part of AME's strategy was to build critical thinking and analytic skills across the organization. Toward that end, AME created and deployed a certification programme for evaluation skills. Their efforts have been successful. Attendees developed awareness and built skills for gathering data for decision making. This programme has played a part in several promotions for past participants. One of the consequences has been that people are talking about data and thinking about measurement when starting new projects. Three full cohorts totalling 33 people have completed the programme and 25 have finished two follow-on projects in order to gain certification. This is the first programme accredited by ISPI.

The leader of the AME group is considering where to take the programme next; the critical component to her decision – determining how the programme will benefit the business most. The programme has already reached 19 employees beyond JetBlue University, and currently there are more than 50 data stewards interested in it. The AME leader is strongly considering a fundamental change to the language of the programme, moving it away from evaluation terminology and closer to the natural business language of JetBlue.

Prediction project

Since 2008, JBU has used Metrics That Matter™ (MTM) as a scalable system to gather training evaluation data across multiple colleges, hundreds of courses and thousands of learners each year. In 2012, the AME group partnered with the CEB team to optimize the performance of its curricula by determining the key drivers of effectiveness.

Using a year-long sample of JBU's training evaluation data, the CEB team developed three regression models which showed the key drivers of effective training. Three outcomes were predicted, each with its own model:

- Learning effectiveness – the extent to which attendees gained new knowledge and skills from training.

- Application on the job – the extent to which attendees applied new knowledge and skills to the job.

- Job performance – the extent to which training improved performance on the job.

Data from two surveys was used. The first survey, the post-event evaluation, gathered data immediately after attendees finished the programme and asked learners to predict how much learning they would apply and how learning would improve performance. The second survey, a follow-up evaluation, gathered data 60 days after training, and asked learners to estimate how much learning they actually applied and how much it actually improved performance. Regression models were created using both the post-event and follow-up data.

Figure 2.5 provides a visual example of one of the prediction models. In this example, the three of the 20+ evaluation measures from the post-event survey are significant predictors of improved job performance. The R^2 values indicate the amount of variance accounted for by the predictor. The values beside the arrows leading from the predictors to the outcome are the unstandardized beta weights. This model indicates that three factors contribute to expected improvement in job performance: 1) gaining new knowledge and skills; 2) belief that those skills will be applied on the job; and 3) having an instructor who was knowledgeable about the subject matter.

Figure 2.5 Prediction Model: key drivers of performance improvement

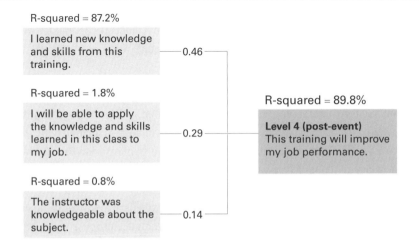

R-squared = 87.2%

I learned new knowledge and skills from this training.

R-squared = 1.8%

I will be able to apply the knowledge and skills learned in this class to my job.

R-squared = 0.8%

The instructor was knowledgeable about the subject.

0.46

0.29

0.14

R-squared = 89.8%

Level 4 (post-event) This training will improve my job performance.

The full prediction equation produced by the regression analysis is provided here:

Level 4 Performance Improvement =
.66 + .46 (I learned new knowledge and skills from this training) +
.29 (I will be able to apply the knowledge and skills learned in this class
to my job) + .14 (The instructor was knowledgeable about the subject)

Here's how to use it. If a learner provides ratings of 4, 3 and 5 respectively for the predictors in the equation, the expected performance improvement score is $(.66 + .46 (4) + .29 (3) + .14 (5)) = 4.07$. Using the equation above, it is clear that high values for each of the items on the left side lead to a high value for performance. Low values for key drivers lead to low predicted performance values.

The value of this predictive model is not in the actual maths of predicting outcomes. It comes from two things: prioritization and comparison – both assist in the continuous improvement process:

- Prioritization: among the more than 20 measures collected on the post-event evaluation survey, the analysis selected the three measures that have the greatest unique influence on the outcome – performance improvement. If performance improvement is low, the course needs improvement. In this case, the L&D team should look to the three drivers in the model first because they are more strongly related to performance improvement than any other factors.

- Comparison helps with prioritization and leads to action. Because resources are limited, it is impossible to improve every course. Benchmarks provide points of comparison and help L&D professionals determine whether a course needs improvement. Courses that are at or above benchmarks – especially for the primary outcome (eg training will improve my job performance) and the three predictors identified – do not require improvement. Those that fall below benchmarks are strong candidates for improvement.

In order to make appropriate comparisons, the CEB team created a template for the AME team which contained the predictors, benchmark values and a final column to insert course scores. The scores provided in Table 2.2 are bogus for illustrative purposes. The course score for Job Impact is below benchmark $(4.88 < 5.57)$. The others are above their respective benchmarks. Based on this simple table, continuous improvement efforts should focus on making the training more applicable in order to improve performance. Despite the complexity of the analysis, the decision making is simple. Chapter 3 explains in more detail the value of a learning analytics system that can automate predictive processes.

Table 2.2 Benchmark comparison table

Category	Item	Benchmark value	Course scores
Learning effectiveness	I learned new knowledge and skills from this training.	5.50	5.89
Job impact	I will be able to apply the knowledge and skills learned in this class to my job.	5.57	**4.88**
Instructor	The Instructor was knowledgeable about the subject.	5.68	5.85

The CEB team also provided a second tool for the AME team – a document with recommendations for improving training. Table 2.3 shows a sample of the key drivers and suggestions for improvement. If a key driver is underperforming based on the benchmark values, the AME team could search for that driver on the left side of Table 2.3 in order to find suggestions for improvement on the right. For example, if the evaluation results indicated that the course needs to improve in the area of course objectives, then the instructional design team should find this key driver 'course objectives' in the left-hand column. In the right-hand column, the team would find recommendations for improving that aspect of training.

Finally, as the AME team sought improvements, the CEB team recommended that they seek balance. Often, efforts to increase effectiveness (eg learning, application and performance) lead to expected increases in outcomes (eg increased customer satisfaction, increased sales, increased revenue). They may also impact efficiency. The extra cost to improve effectiveness (eg guest speakers, simulation software), may decrease substantially the efficiency (eg cost/learner) of the course. Cost-effective training tends to find the right balance among efficiency, effectiveness and outcomes to optimize improvement efforts. Chapter 8 explains the interaction between efficiency, effectiveness and outcomes within the context of Talent Development Reporting Principles. Chapter 7 provides additional examples of continuous improvement efforts using benchmarks.

Table 2.3 Key driver analysis: improvement recommendations table

Key Driver	Suggestions to improve responses to this factor
Course objectives	Align the materials to the course objectives; clearly describe the objectives; provide examples of course materials, topics and objectives to help learners determine if the course is what they need. Ensure truth in advertising. If the course description indicates there will be opportunities to practise and master skills in class, then live up to the promise; provide practice and feedback periods. Do not 'bait and switch', where practice is advertised but lecture is the only learning method. Ensure opportunities to demonstrate and build knowledge and skills on the outlined course objectives – tying the activities to the objectives.
Pace of the course	**Engage the learner by providing a challenging pace** – especially with web-based and other online learning, where they can review or ask questions. More often than not with training, the pace is somewhat to substantially too slow for learners. Generally, with a knowledgeable population, faster is going to be better. **Images:** Methodologies, process and graphs convey substantially more information in a fraction of the time than written or verbal descriptions. Emphasize the use of images rather than words. Information that is supplemented with images is also memorable for a longer period of time. **Self-directed learning:** Self-paced action and discovery (eg clicking various components of a methodology to learn more about it) is a better learning experience than listening to an audio description.
Instructor effectiveness	**Prepare the instructor**: Preparedness for online instruction is just as important for online learning as for instructor-led training. Get instructors familiar and comfortable teaching and trouble shooting in a virtual environment. Prepare the instructors to use various instructional strategies (lecture, discussion, visuals, etc). **Interconnections**: A strong instructor will adjust many aspects of the course to benefit the learner, such as speeding up the pace or slowing it down according to the learners' needs. **Know the audience**: Encourage the instructors to learn about the group that they will be training. This will help with cases referenced, examples, and instructional strategy preparation. **'Experts' as instructors**: Participants want to know that experts in the industry are training them on the topic. Ratings will fall if the instructors are teaching outside of their field of expertise.

Conclusion

Measurement models provide guidance for practitioners who are responsible for evaluating the impact of training. Yet the availability of choice often poses a challenge. Which approach should be used? How often should courses be measured? What tools and processes are needed to effectively measure programmes?

These seemingly simple questions have complex answers that vary per organization and even within business units. The most frequently used approach to measurement is Kirkpatrick's Four Levels of Evaluation, followed by Phillips' ROI Methodology. Research by the American Society for Training and Development (ASTD) in 2004 provides some insight into how often organizations measure each level of evaluation. Figure 2.6 displays results from ASTD's *2004 State of the Industry Report*[38] and a telecommunications company.[15]

Figure 2.6 shows that nearly three-quarters of all organizations measure Level 1, but fewer than one-third measure higher levels. As the level goes up, the percentage of organizations measuring that level goes down. Results for the telecommunications company featured in the figure show the percentage of courses within the curriculum that were measured at each level. Compared to all other companies, this company chose to measure a higher percentage of its courses at the higher levels, but, notably, the pattern is the same. As the level goes up, the percentage of courses measured goes down. This is due to the time, effort and cost associated with evaluating at higher levels and the fact that not every course merits an in-depth Level 4 analysis. A strategic, visible, costly programme – like a series of courses designed to launch a new sales approach – warrants an extensive evaluation including impact on behaviours and business outcome measures, but a 15-minute e-learning course during onboarding that provides instruction about laptop security does not.

It may seem odd to share results here that are more than a decade old. We have done so for two reasons. First, Figure 2.6 shows a pattern. As the level goes up, the percentage of organizations collecting the information goes down. Second, it is important to compare the results in Figure 2.6 to Figure 2.1. The results from CEB's study in 2014 (Figure 2.1) show that more organizations are gathering data at higher levels (eg Levels 2 – ROI) now than in 2004, but the pattern remains the same. Organizations continue to struggle with measuring impact, performance and ROI.

Figure 2.6 Typical application of the Four Levels of Evaluation

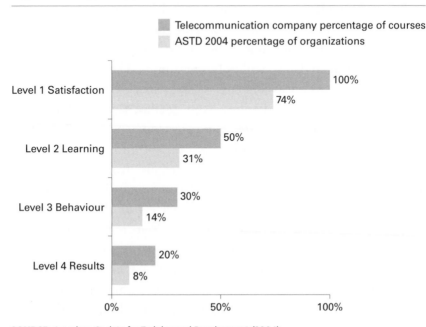

SOURCE: American Society for Training and Development (2004)

CEB's team offers additional guidance when considering how deeply to measure courses. In Figure 2.7, the pyramid represents the proportion of the curriculum that should be evaluated in various ways. For a majority of the curriculum (80 per cent), a standard robust approach should be used that gathers feedback on Levels 1 and 2 while also gathering evidence for Levels 3 – ROI. This can be done using MTM's SmartSheets, which will be discussed later. When standards and tools are in place, a well-designed evaluation system like MTM can scale the evaluation model (Kirkpatrick, Phillips, Bersin, etc) across the organization regardless of which model is applied.

For the remaining two levels of the pyramid (top 20 per cent), the CEB team recommends conducting customized impact studies, which differ from the bottom 80 per cent in two ways. First, these evaluation efforts include multiple methods for gathering data (eg surveys,

Figure 2.7 Strategic application of evaluation resources

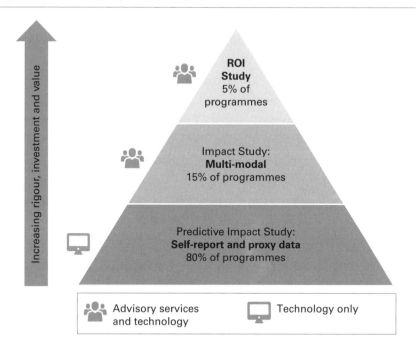

interviews and business data) and emphasize the use of logic models to connect training efforts to individual performance and business measures. The highest level of the pyramid emphasizes ROI as an outcome and includes the monetization of costs and benefits associated with the training programmes. Second, the ability to customize the evaluation process usually requires at least one consultant – an advisor who can guide learning leaders, manage the project and analyse and report the results in alignment with client needs. Some organizations such as HP, Stryker and KPMG among many others have internal consultants like JetBlue's Assessment, Measurement and Evaluation group that can plan and conduct impact studies as part of the evaluation strategy for the corporate university. Organizations that lack such expertise in-house often hire evaluators to do this work.

Now that we have established an understanding of the standard models that are deployed to evaluate training, it is time to transition to the tools that make evaluation possible on a grand scale – in particular, web-based technology systems that gather, store, analyse and report evaluation information.

Endnotes

1 CEB (2014) L&D Leadership Council: Quick Poll Results, internal CEB report.

2 23 John R Mattox II (2010) Extracting value from learning analytics data, KnowledgeAdvisors Webinar, December.

3 PwC (2012) 15th Annual Global CEO Survey [online] https://www. pwc.com/gx/en/ceo-survey/pdf/15th-global-pwc-ceo-survey.pdf, p 23.

4 CEB (2013) Corporate Leadership Council: Working with the Board Survey, internal CEB report.

5 Association for Talent Development (2014) *2014 State of the Industry Report*, Association for Talent Development.

6 Jack Phillips and Patti Phillips (2010) How executives view learning metrics, *Chief Learning Officer*, 3 December [online] http://www. clomedia.com/articles/how-executives-view-learning-metrics.

7 Office of Planning, Research and Evaluation (2010) Chapter 2: What is Program Evaluation? *The Program Manager's Guide to Evaluation*, 2nd edn, p 7, US Department of Health and Human Services, Administration for Children and Families [online] http://www.acf.hhs. gov/sites/default/files/opre/program_managers_guide_to_eval2010.pdf.

8 Peter Rossi and Howard Freeman (1993) *Evaluation: A systematic approach*, 2nd edn, Sage Publications, Newbury Park, CA.

9 William R Shadish, T D Cook and L C Leviton (1991) *Foundations of Program Evaluation: Theories of practice*, Sage Publications, Newbury Park, CA.

10 M David Merrill (2002) First principles of instruction, *Educational Technology Research & Development*, 50 (3) [online] http://mdavidmerrill.com/Papers/firstprinciplesbymerrill.pdf.

11 Robert Gagné (1985) *The Conditions of Learning and the Theory of Instruction*, 4th edn, Holt, Rinehart and Winston, New York.

12 Robert Maribe Branch (2009) *Instructional Design: The ADDIE approach*, Springer, New York.

13 36 37 Shawn Overcast, Therese Schmidt, Kimfong Lei, Carrie Rodgers and Nigel Chung (2009) A case example of assessment and evaluation: building capability in a corporate university, *Performance Improvement*, 48 (6), July.

14 20 Donald Kirkpatrick (1998) *Evaluating Training Programs: The Four Levels*, 2nd edn, Berrett-Koehler Publishers, San Francisco, CA.

15 24 39 Jack Phillips (1997) *Return on Investment in Training and Performance Improvement Programs*, Gulf Publishing Company, Houston, TX.

16 26 Josh Bersin (2008) *The Training Measurement Book: Best practices, proven methodologies, and practical approaches*, Pfeiffer, San Francisco, CA.

17 27 29 Robert Brinkerhoff (2003) *The Success Case Method: Find out quickly what's working and what's not*, Berrett-Koehler Publishers, San Francisco, CA.

18 30 Judith Hale (2002) *Performance-Based Evaluation: Tools and techniques to measure the impact of training*, John Wiley, San Francisco, CA.

19 Donald Kirkpatrick (1956) How to start an objective evaluation of your training program, *The Journal of the American Society of Training Directors*, May–June.

21 Donald Kirkpatrick and James Kirkpatrick (2005) *Transferring Learning to Behaviors: Using the Four Levels to improve performance*, Berrett-Koehler Publishers, San Francisco, CA.

22 Donald Kirkpatrick and James Kirkpatrick (2007) *Implementing the Four Levels: A Practical guide for implementing the Four Levels of Evaluation*, Berrett-Koehler Publishers, San Francisco, CA.

25 Paula Ketter (2010) The best of measuring and evaluating learning, *T+D Magazine*, American Society for Training and Development, pp 1–16, December.

28 Robert O Brinkerhoff (2005) The Success Case Method: a strategic evaluation approach to increasing the value and effect of training, *Advances in Developing Human Resources*, 7 (1), p 91.

31 Judith Hale (2012) *Performance-Based Certification: How to define a valid, defensible, cost-effective program*, 2nd edn, John Wiley, San Francisco, CA.

32 Sharon Shrock and William Coscarelli (2007) *Criterion-Referenced Test Development: Technical and legal guidelines for corporate training*, Berrett-Koehler Publishers, San Francisco, CA.

33 Steven J Osterlind (1998) *Constructing Test Items: Multiple-choice, constructed-response, performance and other formats*, Kluwer Academic Publishers Group, Massachusetts.

34 JetBlue: http://en.wikipedia.org/wiki/JetBlue.

35 International Society for Performance Improvement: http://en.wikipedia. org/wiki/International_Society_for_Performance_Improvement.

38 American Society for Training and Development (2004) *2004 State of the Industry Report*, ASTD.

Access to the CEB resources cited in this book is limited to members. For information about membership, please contact CEB's Member Support Centre at CEB.Support@cebglobal.com or +1-866-913-2632.

Technology's role in learning measurement 03

Imagination fuelled the science fiction stories that have entertained audiences for decades – sometimes centuries. Jules Verne wrote about travelling the globe in 80 days and exploring underwater in a fantastical submarine. He even described travel through space and time.

What was once science fiction is now science fact. Nuclear submarines spend weeks underwater. Airlines allow us to travel around the globe in less than 48 hours, and Wi-Fi on the plane allows you to watch movies that stream to your laptop. The SpaceX project is exploring commercial space travel as a way to shorten global travel times, and space travel in general seems mundane.

Technology makes fiction fact. Clearly, science plays a crucial role. New materials like titanium and carbon fibre make planes lighter and faster. Engineering and design principles help shape the wings and improve the power of the jet engines. Yet, electronic technology seems the most amazing of all. The manual mechanisms for steering a plane from the cockpit are redundant. The autopilot feature controls the plane by wire, sending signals to ailerons and engines faster and more effectively than pilots. On the Boeing 787, wireless technology also enables a self-monitoring diagnostic system to send data to ground-based technicians. It can also predict mechanical problems before they happen.

Technology systems also bring innovation, effectiveness and efficiency to the business world. Simple innovations like bar codes and scanners changed the retail industry. Enterprise resource planning systems (ERPs) from Oracle and SAP enabled the tracking and management of employees and other business resources. Salesforce.com has standardized the sales process and made it more efficient using cloud-based technology. Technology is transforming the way we do business, including the way we manage learning events and evaluate them.

What should technology do?

Technology enables business processes. It makes great leaps forward in our ability to do things faster and better. More specifically, it creates efficiencies, increases productivity, changes our world view, helps solve problems and makes businesses more effective. Here are some examples:

- **Increasing efficiency**
  Technology allows us to do more with less, eliminate mistakes and avoid the boredom associated with routine tasks that require little to no brain power. At the simplest level, consider the bill-counting machine at a local bank. In seconds, it can process a stack of $20 notes and return a total count and value. On a more complex level, consider the millions of transactions that occur at Walmart stores around the world. The barcode scanners are faster and more accurate than cashiers. Moreover, the point-of-sale system (POS) uploads and aggregates the sales data for that register, and shares it with a cloud-based database that records every transaction from that register, every register in that store and every store around the world. As a result of the technology, a variety of business processes such as profit calculations, tax accounting and logistics planning are much more efficient.

- **Increasing productivity**
  Productivity increases when certain tasks are done faster. Technology also helps organizations do tasks better. Going back to the cash-counting machine, one of the common errors that bank tellers make is incorrectly counting cash. The counting machines make the process more efficient, *and* they are more accurate. Increased efficiency and increased accuracy are a sweet spot for improving

productivity. Software packages like Excel, Lotus Notes and Hyperion were designed to increase productivity within the field of finance by making data processing more accurate and efficient. Likewise, online trading sites like Bloomberg, eTrade, Scottrade and many others provide rich information about publicly traded companies. The analytic engines that power these sites perform complex analysis in seconds and display results in the form of time series graphs with confidence intervals, Bollinger bands, risk ratios and other metrics. The information provided helps investors make trading decisions. By presenting complex information, these trading companies make individual investors more productive because they can quickly make informed decisions about buying and trading stocks. Consequently, the trading companies also become more productive. Instead of forcing investors to work through a broker, the trading companies facilitate the trading process using the Internet and make money on each trade.

- **Changing the world / solving problems**
  More than 125 years ago, one simple invention accelerated productivity during the industrial revolution. The light bulb changed the world. Productivity was no longer subject to ambient light. It allowed employees to work before and after sunrise without candles or gas lights. Today, many manufacturing facilities still run three eight-hour shifts every day to maintain 24 hours of daily productivity. The light bulb also facilitated greater exploration of our world, whether it was in the deep, lightless salt mines beneath Kansas or the vast darkness of the ocean floor. Innovation helps us do something new or differently. The iPhone allows us to talk to each other face to face, take pictures, play video games and even light our way when a light bulb isn't handy.

In the world of learning analytics, innovation arrived in the form of learning management systems, testing/assessment tools, evaluation tools, and e-learning and webinar platforms. These technologies have transformed the way corporate universities train their professionals. We'll explore the evaluation aspects in more detail throughout the rest of the chapter.

Benefits and costs of learning technologies

The value of technology systems is monitored closely because the benefits can uplift an entire workforce but they can also cripple a budget. When weighing the benefits and costs of systems, the C-suite often focuses on a simple metric: Return on Investment (ROI). All of the benefits mentioned in the last section are quantifiable. They have measurable value. A code scanner can allow a cashier to handle 5 to 10 times as many customers per hour. A logistics system can minimize the costs of storage in warehouses because goods are shipped directly from the producer to the retail location. Notably, the benefits of technology also have measurable costs, including the technology itself, the cost to install it and the cost to train employees to use it.

Some tools have massive intrinsic value – so much so that the obvious benefits outweigh the necessary costs, even when the costs are substantial. When e-mail first became widely available in the late 1980s and early 1990s, business leaders had to estimate the time savings that would be realized from instant communication, reduction in paper and the ability to transfer documents from one employee to another across the globe. They also had to weigh the actual costs of the software, security issues, deployment, training, employee resistance and the eventual shift in culture that comes with game-changing technology. When searching for the ROI estimate, the costs and barriers to implementation often seem to outweigh the benefits.

In 1962, Everett Roger introduced his theory on the diffusion of innovation.[1] According to the theory, early adopters of technology tend to be risk-taking visionaries who can see the tangible and intangible value that others cannot (or they just want to be first to use a new and interesting tool that has cache). Late adopters are risk avoiders; they only purchase new technology when it has proven its value. Ironically, by the time late adopters begin using the 'new' technology, often it has advanced by multiple versions and is considered 'old' by early adopters. Figure 3.1 shows a normal distribution and how innovations diffuse throughout the population.[2]

In hindsight, some tools, like a phone, a fax machine, e-mail or the Internet, have such extensive and obvious value that the day-to-day business world would seem prehistoric without them. Their value for

Figure 3.1 Diffusion of innovations curves

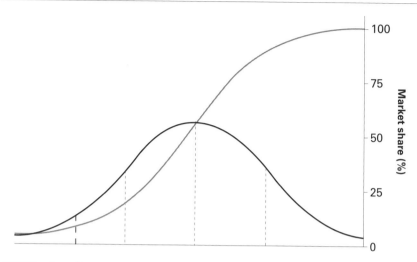

SOURCE: adapted from Rogers (1962/2003)

one person in one role could be substantially different from the value for another person in another role, but the value remains positive. When the utility and value of a tool become so pervasive that the culture is dependent upon it, its value is no longer scrutinized. The value is accepted as common knowledge and eventually becomes conventional wisdom.

Today, common knowledge dictates that a college education is a worthwhile investment. Jobs are easier to obtain with an undergraduate degree; career growth and earning power also increase. Likewise, graduate and professional degrees make more profitable careers possible, such as physicians, litigators and corporate leaders. Not so long ago, this common knowledge was not so common. In the late 1960s and early 1970s, Gary Becker set about testing the value of a college education by searching for a definitive answer to the question, 'Is a college education worth the investment?' Using information collected from the census and other government reports about economic measures across the country, Becker demonstrated that a college education does in fact lead to greater earning power and greater economic stability. Becker's book *Human Capital*[3] comprehensively examines this question. His research in this area was so profound and valuable that he received a Nobel Prize for Economics in 1992.[4]

Margaret Thatcher, the former prime minister of the United Kingdom, put Becker's notions into practice with a country-wide experiment. She broke the control of local school systems by offering funding at a national level and exercised more control over the learning provided with a nationalized curriculum. She approved the creation of more comprehensive schools – an open-enrolment secondary school for learners between the ages of 11 and 16 years – than any other secretary of state before or since.[5] She provided higher education to the masses and enabled the rapid growth and prosperity of a middle class, jumpstarting a stagnant British economy. By supplying businesses with a talented workforce, she fuelled the country's economic engine.[6]

Becker also investigated the value of talent development programmes (training).[7] His research indicates that development programmes are certainly valuable and they have a positive Return on Investment. Despite his fundamental research, his award-winning analysis of development programmes does not satisfy those business leaders who want to know if their unique curricula, including specific courses, help the organization achieve business goals.

The value of a college education and talent development programmes is well documented by Becker, yet there is an odd split of opinions about their value within the business world. One perspective, based on conventional wisdom, indicates that development programmes work. Anyone who has been to a good learning event knows that it has value. Yet, the other perspective is driven by lingering doubts and the need to prove value. The first perspective is often given voice in this way: 'Of course training works. If it didn't, we wouldn't pay for it.' The voice of the contrarian perspective asks, 'Well, how do we know? Has it been measured?'

Unfortunately, rigorous evaluation processes are not easy to implement and they are costly. When evaluators share the complex and costly methods used to assess the impact of learning events, business leaders sometimes revert to the first perspective, 'We know it works, so we don't have to measure it', so they don't have to spend valuable time, human resources and money on complex evaluation.

Today, the challenge is to apply the rigorous scientific methods of evaluation in a cost-effective, scalable way. Technology is the key.

The companies that see the value of investing in tools like laptops, software, mobile phones, Internet access, apps, etc, assume the risk in terms of costs, change management, disgruntled employees, training, process change and culture shifts. They also reap the rewards of faster speed to market, more efficient processes, more accurate output and intangible benefits like innovation and engaged employees.

This is where informed risk and decision making lead to competitive advantage for companies.

Business leaders, particularly the CEO and CFO, are constantly looking for the next piece of technology that can transform the business. It is their responsibility to drive profits by finding the people, processes and tools that will decrease costs and increase productivity. Together they manage the corporate strategy by selectively investing in operational initiatives.

Are they able to conduct ROI studies on every new process or tool that is available? Certainly not, but they do rely on directors and managers to discover the next new thing that will make the business better. Those directors and managers must also bring a business case forward which should answer questions like, 'What is the cost of the next new thing?' and 'What are the expected benefits?' Each year during the annual budgeting cycle, the business leaders consider the panoply of next new things from every business unit, and they must choose which aligns to business goals and will create the most competitive advantage. Shockingly, the intelligence that underpins the ROI analysis varies widely. Some new tools are fully vetted with highly reliable and valid ROI information because the tool is widely used across the industry and hundreds of case studies demonstrate its value. Others come with a gut-feel recommendation from a senior manager who believes in his heart of hearts that the new tool will solve the problem.

Dave Vance, former president of Caterpillar University and current executive director of the Center for Talent Reporting, shared the following story about ROI in his book, *The Business of Learning*.[8] While at Caterpillar, leaders considered new and innovative ways to build earth-moving products that provided substantial margins.

If a new process for building a bulldozer was expected to yield an ROI of 25 per cent ($1.25 for every dollar invested), leaders often considered the approach valuable enough to pursue. In contrast, Vance often found ROI values for development programmes that exceeded 100 per cent. When he presented his findings to leadership, the C-suite thought he had misplaced a decimal – that the ROI was 10 per cent not 100 per cent. He had not. Such high ROI values are reasonable for a programme. Phillips has documented ROI values that exceed 250 per cent.[9] These ROI values reflect the power of development to increase productivity, to transform thinking and to solve problems. Yet, the C-suite did not find Vance's ROI values credible. They scrutinized the Phillips' ROI Methodology[10] that Vance applied, and they insisted on a reassessment. Vance worked with his colleagues, fellow economists, who were responsible for computing ROI values for earth-moving products and found that the methods for calculating benefits and costs were somewhat different for products than for training. Eventually, Vance adjusted his approach to create a modified metric called Return on Learning (ROL). For decision-making purposes, a development programme that provided a 30 per cent ROL was considered realistic, achievable and worth the investment by the C-suite.

This example highlights one of the primary functions of the chief learning officer (CLO) – to inform the CEO, CFO and other leaders about the investment that is being made to develop talent. At the very least the CLO is on the hook to answer the questions, 'How much is being spent on development programmes and how is it being spent?' The CFO wants those answers, and the CEO wants to know, 'Are talent development programmes working?' Additional questions include: 'If it's working, how do you know?', 'Are programmes helping the business achieve its business goals?', 'If not, why not?', 'What needs to be fixed and how can it be fixed?' and 'Should our valuable resources be spent on other things (eg processes, talent, tools) that might provide a better return?'

The CLO gathers information to answer these questions from many sources. Some CLOs simply walk the halls after programmes to hear the buzz about courses. Others solicit feedback from attendees, instructors or managers who oversee the performance of attendees.

While these approaches provide information, they lack rigour and scale and they tend to be biased. Some CLOs have the good fortune to have an evaluation team that is responsible for systematically gathering feedback, summarizing it and reporting it in aggregate. Others cannot afford this valuable asset.

An evaluation team, whether large or small, requires technology to enable the evaluation process. This is often the case with large learning and development functions that offer hundreds or thousands of courses. Technology is needed to execute evaluation processes at scale – gathering data through web-based survey tools, analysing data or creating summative reports through technology applications. These features make large-scale evaluation possible.

Within L&D departments, evaluation is typically handled in one of three ways:

- **Talent development programmes are not evaluated**
  The learning and development team does not evaluate their programmes. Instructional designers prefer to create and deploy courses; they may not have the skills or the resources to evaluate the courses they create. These L&D departments are blind to the success and failure of courses. Moreover, they cannot help the CLO inform the C-suite about the value that learning programmes bring to the business.

- **Programmes are evaluated internally**
  In these departments, a team of analysts is tasked with the responsibility of developing the measurement strategy, building evaluations, deploying them to gather data, analysing results and reporting outcomes to stakeholders. The case study section of this chapter provides a detailed description of three internal evaluation teams and how technology changed their structure and processes over time.

- **Evaluation is outsourced**
  Rather than build a team of analysts internally, some organizations choose to hire a vendor and thus outsource the evaluation process.

What's most interesting though is how technology is changing the possibilities for evaluating programmes. The case study in this chapter will show how technology has reduced the size of evaluation teams within corporate universities. Equally important, technology enables L&D groups to grow their evaluation capabilities by starting with one full-time employee or even one person with half of their responsibilities aligned to measurement. Before discussing how technology enables the evaluation process, it is important to consider the criteria for a technology tool that help it provide value.

What are the requirements for any new technology system in the business intelligence space?

Business intelligence (BI) systems represent a unique set of technology tools in the digital world. BI systems typically focus on the analysis and reporting of data. They bring efficiency to business processes by automating manual processes such as distribution, collection, analysis, reporting and communication. The primary value of BI systems is to provide insight; they must transform data into information for decision making. Useful BI tools do the following critical tasks:

- Process data – they use simple analytic routines to summarize the data using descriptive and inferential statistics.

- Report results – they create static (unchanging) reports and dynamic (changing) reports like dashboards, that are regularly updated with data.

- Prescribe next steps – they provide recommended actions based on the results.

- Accessibility – they put information in the hands of the end users for decision making.

BI tools tend to process data after it has been collected, but some tools can also perform the data collection, storage and classification of data prior to analysis.

At this point it is worthwhile to differentiate between two types of information: descriptive and evaluative. Descriptive information reflects a record of what has happened. A restaurant receipt is descriptive because it records the cost, payment method, amount paid and change if needed. Evaluative information summarizes a set of data and conveys a point of view or value – providing a judgement as to whether the data is good or bad. A monthly financial statement for a restaurant is descriptive because it shows the inflow of revenue and the outflow of expenses. It becomes evaluative when it is compared to a monthly target. Was the monthly revenue goal reached? It may even show a trend across months for the year and compare monthly results to the same month last year. Comparisons provide evaluative information.

A simpler example of evaluative results comes from Netflix. The five-star rating system provided by viewers allows other subscribers to see if others liked the movie. Netflix also provides a list of recommended movies to subscribers based on past ratings. The analytics engine on the Netflix website crunches evaluation data and provides information that users can act upon. In this way, Netflix uses a BI system that helps build revenue; by recommending movies that subscribers will enjoy, it helps create a positive customer experience that leads to continued subscriptions.

What types of data are descriptive in the learning and development industry? There are many. Transactional data tends to be descriptive; this includes data related to learning activities, learning modality and cost such as the number of people trained, the learning method and the cost per learner. Learning management systems are primarily descriptive – focused just on the number of transactions processed through the system. The core functions offered by these descriptive systems include the storage and deployment of information (eg courses), personnel profiles, compliance information, learner histories and learning paths. As the name describes, these systems manage learner data. Their core function is not evaluative.

What types of data are evaluative in the learning and development industry? Evaluation surveys, tests and business outcome data are evaluative. Evaluations are most often surveys that gather opinions from learners about the quality of the programme, whether attendees learned knowledge and skills, whether they intend to apply their learning and whether application will improve their performance.

Focus groups and interviews can also be used to gather qualitative information for evaluation purposes, but they are not as scalable as surveys. Tests, particularly the combined use of pre- and post-course exams, provide information about how much knowledge and skills learners acquired from programmes. Business data such as sales, customer satisfaction and revenue can be influenced by development programmes and should be evaluated to show impact.

Notably, some learning management systems gather evaluative information. Some have assessment tools which gather performance information – typically test scores – for learners before and after programmes. Some also have built-in evaluation tools that gather opinions from learners about the quality of programme. As learning management systems advance, they will incorporate features that gather evaluative information for decision making. Table 3.1 shows CEB's current and future approach to measurement, as well as associated

Table 3.1 Current and future state of training evaluation

	Current state	Future state	Benefit
Metrics	Volume, Cost, Satisfaction	Efficiency, Effectiveness, Outcomes	Comprehensive view of learning impact
Source	Learner	Learner, Instructor, Manager, Business data	Triangulate perspectives to uncover gaps and demonstrate value
Timing	After learning	After learning and on the Job	Identify drivers of scrap that occur outside talent development programmes
Benchmarks	Internal	Internal and External	Prioritize improvements based on comparison to competitors
Process	Manually intensive	Highly automated	Scale measurements to be consistent and have significant impact across the enterprise

benefits. The first row focuses on metrics and reflects the fact that most organizations collect efficiency information and some effectiveness information (eg satisfaction with learning). In the future, three types of measures will be gathered and used to evaluate development programmes: efficiency, effectiveness and outcomes. The last row of the table is also worth noting here. Technology will make evaluative data more available and require less manual intervention to analyse and report it.

CASE STUDY   How has technology influenced training evaluation in L&D functions?

As an industry, professional services firms provide highly valuable skills and insights to business clients, typically in the form of auditing, tax and business advisory services. If the industry label does not sound familiar, some brand names might, such as McKinsey, Accenture, PwC, KPMG, Deloitte, EY and Booz Allen Hamilton. These businesses depend on the quality of their people to serve their client needs. For these firms, exceptional corporate universities with outstanding development programmes provide an enticing lure for college graduates and experienced hires. They also provide critical knowledge and skills in a complex, highly regulated and constantly changing business environment. Each year, these organizations spend hundreds of millions of dollars training professionals across all levels. The Association for Talent Development (ATD) indicates that the average spend per employee is roughly $1,200 per person per year when averaged across all organizations.[11] Professional services firms typically spend three to four times that amount annually per person in the United States.

As one might expect, the firm leaders want to know whether their investment in training is effective. Government agencies that regulate these firms do as well. Federal and state regulators require that all training be evaluated if it is going to provide continuing professional education credits (CPEs). Auditors and tax professionals need to complete a minimum number of CPEs each year to maintain their professional licences. In this way, regulations push the L&D departments to create quality training to help professionals to stay current in their fields.

In response to the requirement to evaluate training, some of these firms have exceptionally good evaluation teams. The size and responsibilities of each team vary but every firm maintains compliance by evaluating training. Additionally, those teams provide useful information to instructional designers about what is working within the curriculum and what is not. When something is broken, the evaluation team provides suggestions for improvement based on the data collected.

For three of these firms, technology has dramatically impacted the evaluation teams and their processes. This case study focuses on the impact of technology over a 12-year period from 1998 to 2010. In 1998, one firm maintained a corporate university and brought its partners and employees to the training centre regularly for development. It was common to train hundreds of new hires each week for 2–4 weeks at a time. With such large, costly courses, the firm wanted to know if their programmes were effectively transferring knowledge and skills. To that end, the organization created a rather large measurement and assessment group – roughly 35 people strong – to evaluate courses. Group members had a variety of skills aligned to specific roles. There was a group of measurement experts who designed and executed evaluation plans for strategic programmes. Another group of Lotus Notes experts created surveys and managed the data collection and reporting platform for a majority of the courses. There was also a handful of statisticians who used SPSS, Excel and Access to analyse data. The team evaluated every programme, including classes that were being deployed as virtual instructor-led courses, video courses and self-paced web-based programmes. For instructor-led classes, Lotus Notes was a useful tool because it provided a platform for creating training content, allowed for in-class exams to be built into the content, provided immediate feedback about student performance on those exams and provided end-of-course evaluations that could be deployed by e-mail. Results were captured, analysed and reported within Lotus Notes. Due to organizational downsizing, the team eventually shrank from 35 to 20 people between 1998 and 2002.

As one firm downsized its evaluation function, another increased its function. Viewing measurement as a critical component of the L&D function, the leaders of the corporate university formalized its measurement team with a leader who could manage its measurement of people, tools and processes. The full team consisted of two managers and eight temps, who used Lotus Notes to support evaluation services. Knowledge testing became a priority, and the firm deployed a testing and assessment system as a tool to manage tests. As expected, this tool worked well for tests, but not so well for evaluations. The system gathered data well, but it did not have the out-of-the-box reporting capabilities necessary to meet the evaluation needs of the L&D team.

The firm continued to search for a capable evaluation system to replace Lotus Notes, and KnowledgeAdvisors' Metrics That Matter™ (MTM) system became a leading candidate. Eventually, the IT team and L&D leadership decided it was the only system that could meet business requirements, including: standardizing the data collection process, scaling to meet the variable volume of programmes, reaching nearly 30,000 employees across the United States (and occasionally other countries), and providing out-of-the-box reporting to meet the needs of the learning community.

To make the MTM system efficient, it was integrated with the learning management system. In this way, MTM received all of the necessary course and participant information required to send automated e-mails to learners, instructors and managers with links to evaluation forms. The system also allowed the evaluation team to run reports manually or schedule them to run automatically on a set date. Automated reports could also be sent by the system to preselected stakeholders by e-mail. Efficiencies gained by using the system in the evaluation processes changed the group. Within four years the total number of temps was reduced from eight to three, and a new evaluator was hired – someone who could focus on conducting advanced statistical analysis and ROI studies for critical programmes.

In 2006 a third firm decided to grow its measurement capabilities within its US learning and development practice by hiring an evaluation expert to lead a team entirely dedicated to evaluating talent development programmes. The team assumed many of the measurement responsibilities that had been distributed among instructional designers and delivery personnel. Effective evaluation processes were already in place, but the processes were time consuming and onerous for professionals who had little interest or expertise in evaluation. The resident evaluation system was a modification of a system designed as a testing platform. While the system proved capable as a testing tool, it fell short as an evaluation tool. With the help of the L&D IT team, the measurement team defined its requirements for an evaluation system. The Metrics That Matter™ (MTM) system was selected for the corporate university and implemented to handle the distribution, data collection, analysis and reporting needs. From 2006 to 2010, the measurement team grew from one person to four. Using MTM and the aforementioned testing platform, they were able to serve the evaluation needs of the four major business units in the United States which trained more than 30,000 people annually. Because MTM did so much of the evaluation work with regards to distribution of surveys, data collection, analysis and reporting, the measurement team was able to focus on other valuable measurement issues for the learning and development group, including ROI studies, research questions (eg how much training is needed to improve employee retention?) and needs assessment.

Many factors influenced the effectiveness of the measurement teams at the three firms mentioned above, including external market pressures, changing industry regulations and internal measurement needs. However, one critical influencer was technology, which played a substantial role in adjusting the size and capabilities of the measurement groups across these firms. Figure 3.2 shows the relationship between the size of the evaluation group and use of scalable technologies between 1998 and 2010.

Figure 3.2 Scalable technology and evaluation group size

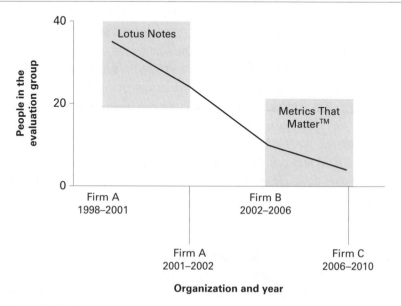

SOURCE: CEB (2016)

Technology also enables science. In order to be effective, evaluation surveys should meet industry standards for validity and reliability. Validity relates to truth: is the survey measuring what it truly intends to measure? Reliability relates to consistency: is the survey gathering similar responses from learners every time it is deployed? These survey characteristics can be tested statistically. In fact, the core questions that contribute to the benchmarks within the Metrics That Matter™ system have been tested and the results are overwhelmingly positive, exceeding validity and reliability standards.[12] Why is this important? Stakeholders sometimes question the value of the self-reported data gathered on surveys. Statistical testing indicates that the results in the MTM system are scientifically sound indicators of the influence of development programmes on learning and performance improvement.

What is the ROI of technology systems?

The example above shows an inverse relationship between the use of technology and group size. As scalable systems are implemented, the size of the evaluation group decreases. As expected, systems make processes more efficient, freeing skilled workers to attend to complex tasks. This example raises the question, what is the ROI of implementing such systems?

To answer the question, it is essential to define the costs and the benefits both before and after the systems are implemented. In this case, if the same work is being accomplished before and after (eg all benefits being equal), then the cost differential determines whether the ROI of the systems is more valuable than the employees. If the cost of the systems is less than the cost of the salaries replaced by the system, then the systems are more cost effective and the ROI is better.

The reality is that systems are much more efficient and accurate than humans, especially for repetitive tasks needed on a massive scale. As such, even costly systems are typically less expensive than the employees assigned the tasks.

Depending on the system, efficiency is only one benefit. Barcode scanning systems make the retail checkout process faster and more accurate. Other systems like predictive analytic tools take transactional data and provide insights heretofore unrealized. Insights, recommendations and financial benefits, not just cost efficiencies, make investments in such technology truly valuable.

In 2012, Nucleus Research examined the cost effectiveness of using predictive analytics and found an ROI of $10.66 for every dollar invested.[13] Even more striking, the analytics deployments with the highest ROI values were distinguished by the way that the systems made data available to decision makers, enabling them to find ways to increase revenue and reduce costs. Interestingly, Corporate Leadership Council's 2013 study of HR analytics revealed diminishing returns for analytics systems as the technology became more sophisticated. The only exceptions were cases where the organization also made parallel improvements in the actionability of the analysis for the business.[14] So systems bring immediate value by making human processes more efficient. In order to bring long-term value, they also need to provide insights that lead to action. In order to provide maximum value to learning organizations, evaluation systems in the learning space should provide both efficiency and insight.

Applying principles of business intelligence systems to learning and development

In order for business intelligence (BI) tools to be valuable, they must convert data into information through analysis, and then they must recommend specific actions. The goal is to put information and recommendations into the hands of the end users quickly so they can make decisions and adjust. Mint.com is a perfect example of such insight – albeit for finance, not L&D. Mint.com gathers individual spending records from credit cards or bank accounts and quickly analyses the data, creating dashboards with spending categories. It provides insights into how much was spent per month and how much might be spent in the coming month. It also makes simple recommendations for saving money such as, 'Avoid paying finance charges by using a credit card that does not charge interest.'

L&D is lagging behind the financial world in terms of predictive analytics systems, but certain companies are making great strides. At Perspectives 2015, Skillsoft's annual conference, Anshul Sheopuri revealed some of the predictive analytics work he had completed for Skillsoft.[15] Sheopuri, a senior manager of digital research at IBM, and his team of data scientists, used learner records, titles, levels and available curricula within Skillsoft to create predictive models for development. The algorithms were designed to determine what courses were needed to fill gaps and advance careers. Rather than show the mathematical models to learners – which would likely be indecipherable – Skillsoft chose to integrate them with the Skillsoft LMS. When a learner enters the LMS, he or she now sees a customized development plan. To advance, learners simply enrol in their next learning opportunity.

Since early 2000, the Metrics That Matter™ system (MTM) has gathered, analysed and reported data for end users. As a BI tool, it provides insight into the two questions that drive most evaluation processes: 'Are my talent development programmes effective?' and 'How can those programmes be improved?' More recently, MTM augmented its BI capabilities by automatically executing more in-system analytics, comparing results to benchmarks and making recommendations that appear effortlessly on a dashboard for users. The following section explains how MTM applies best practices from BI systems to improve decision making for end users with a five-step process: gather data, store and code it, process it, report it and prescribe recommendations:

- **Gather data**
  The MTM system deploys standard web-based surveys at the end of training via e-mail. The surveys can be customized to include specific questions about content, or delivery or organizational issues. However, the value of using standard questions is that the results from the questions can be compared to benchmarks that are based on millions of data points. When MTM is integrated with a learning management system, it makes the distribution process extremely efficient by automatically sending evaluations to participants and instructors the day that training ends. This particularly is valuable when hundreds or thousands of courses need to be evaluated daily. In addition to gathering data via surveys, the system also accepts other data sets through a systematic uploading process (eg file transfer protocol) or manual upload of spreadsheets.

- **Store and code it**
  More than a decade ago, data storage was a critical issue because capacity was limited and costly. Now storage space is abundant and inexpensive even in the Cloud, but it is still valuable to apply best practices because the abundance of data stretches storage capacity. Relational data files tend to be more efficient, with a small number of variables and long columns of data. When classifying data, the MTM system adheres to existing taxonomies such as the Dow Jones Industrials for industry codes and the Association for Talent Development (ATD) codes for course types to ensure data can be classified according to a small number of

standards. These taxonomies also ensure that data can be retrieved, analysed and reported in meaningful ways.

- **Process it**

  Most analytics are routine, repetitive processes with a finite set of steps, making them perfect candidates for automation. The code that creates descriptive statistics such as the mean, standard deviation and frequency distribution is the same whether the data set has 10 cases or 10,000. A survey with one question or 100 can be analysed quickly by the system as long as the data is structured and coded appropriately. An analytics system that processes data with routine scripts within the system is far more efficient than a process that requires an analyst to download the data, format it and then manually conduct an analysis. MTM processes data within the system to create reports. It also executes scheduled routines to automatically update benchmarks to speed up processing time.

- **Report it**

  Two types of reports provide value because they are so efficient: static and dynamic reports. The goal of both is to extract patterns in the data and transform them into information:

  - *Static reports* are out-of-the-box standard documents that are based on routine analytics. This might include the computation and display of the average and response distribution for every quantitative survey question as well as a list of all comments to open-ended questions. A static report is created on demand and can be run multiple times with ease as new data rolls in. See Figure 3.3 for an example of a Quick Question Report from MTM which summarizes the results of survey questions.

  - *Dynamic reports* tend to be graphically based and typically take the form of a dashboard. Results refresh automatically as data rolls in. See Figure 3.4 for an example of a dashboard in MTM.

- **Prescribe recommendations**

  Truly valuable business intelligence systems include some level of interpretation, moving beyond simple reporting to insights. Often this requires a comparison between results and benchmarks or the inclusion of additional data. Logic is also required in the form of if–then reporting. If the results say this, then provide that insight. The MTM system provides prescriptive recommendations with its Instant Insights™ dashboard. The primary metric analysed is scrap learning, which is the amount of training that is wasted because it is not applied on the job. This metric is a useful indicator of training quality and will be discussed in more detail in Chapter 5. The dashboard shows a simple box which displays the scrap rate for the organization and a comparison to the benchmark value. If scrap is lower (better) than the benchmark, the box is green. If scrap is higher (worse) than benchmark, the box is red. This is simple descriptive analysis with dashboard reporting. The dashboard provides insight through in-system analytics. The scrap values across all evaluations for all respondents for all courses in the curriculum are correlated with all other questions on the evaluations to determine which questions influence scrap the most. The top influencer of scrap is shown on the dashboard (eg learning effectiveness) and additional influencers are listed lower on the dashboard. More importantly, the system recognizes which drivers are being displayed and provides a list of recommendations that align to the influencers. Instructional designers can use the influencers as a guide for digging deeper into the data to find root causes of scrap. They can also use the recommendations as a starting point for improving the quality of the course. Figure 3.5 shows an Instant Insights™ dashboard. In this case, scrap is 43 per cent which is worse than (above) the benchmark of 27 per cent and the top influencer is Support Tools. Additional influencers are listed below the recommendations (eg Alignment, Support Tools and Courseware). The estimated value of reducing scrap to the benchmark level is also provided in the box to the right – roughly $4.4 million. These values are calculated using an average salary estimate and a benchmark from the Association for Talent Development (ATD) for average cost of training. These values can be customized for each organization.

In summary, the Instant Insights™ dashboard provides value by identifying a problem (scrap), determining what contributes to scrap, providing recommendations for reducing scrap and estimating the cost savings that can be realized by improving training. In this way,

Figure 3.3 Standard Quick Question Report

METRICS THAT MATTER

Welcome, InnovateU   MTM Help ⊚ | Log Out

| Dashboard | Reporting | Administration | My Settings |

Reporting > My Recent Reports > Quick Question

Find A Report
My Recent Reports
Recommended Reports
Show All Reports

Manage Reports
Schedule Class Reports
Audit Class Reports
Manage Scheduled Reports
View Saved Reports
My Files

Queued Reports

Jul 20, 2015
● [Completed]
Quick Question

Jul 16, 2015
● [Completed]
Courses by Job Impact and
Knowledge Gained

● [Completed]
Learner Comments

Quick Question Query

Report Name:
Quick Question
↻ Update Name

⊙ Help

➜ Data Download   📅 Schedule   ✉ Email   🖨 Print   ✗ Delete
                                📊 Excel   📄 PDF   Move to Folder: ▸

Quick Question

Run By: Admin Innovate U. (InnovateU)
Date Run: Jul 20, 2015

MTM Tool: Quick Question
From Saved Query: No

| Date: | | Instructor(s): | | Course: | Advanced Negotiations |
| Learning Provider: | InnovateU | Location: | | Client: | Irrigation Technologies |

Summary

	N*	1+	2+	3+	4+	5	Average
Business Results	10			20.00%	60.00%	20.00%	4.33
Courseware	10			15.00%	65.00%	20.00%	4.37
Job Impact	10			20.00%	70.00%	10.00%	4.27
Learning Effectiveness	10			40.00%	40.00%	20.00%	4.20
Online Delivery	10			24.49%	51.02%	24.49%	4.33
Return on Investment	10				100.00%		4.33
Support Tools	10			20.00%	60.00%	20.00%	4.33
Summary	10			20.81%	59.73%	19.46%	4.32

Figure 3.4 Dashboard example from Metrics That Matter™

METRICS
THAT MATTER

| Dashboard | Reporting | Administration | My Settings |

Welcome, InnovateU MTM Help ⓘ | Log Out

Learning Effectiveness

Last Published On: May 14, 2015

[Publish] [⚙ Manage]

| Executive Summary | Impact | Operations | Courses | Instructors |

Results and Value Performance Trends ⬜ ⊠

Performance
5.0
4.5
4.0
3.5
3.0
2.5
2.0
1.5
1.0

Jul 31 2014
Aug 31 2014
Sep 30 2014
Oct 31 2014
Nov 30 2014
Dec 31 2014
Jan 31 2015
Feb 28 2015
Mar 31 2015
Apr 30 2015
May 31 2015
Jun 30 2015

● Business Results ◆ Job Impact

View Full Report
Data as of: Jun 30, 2015

Next data refresh: Aug 3, 2015

L&D Net Promoter Score ⬜ ⊠

Tab Actions ▸

Promoters: 24%
Passives: 19%
Detractors: 57%

-33%

Net Promoter
Promoters – Detractors

Benchmark: 52%

View Full Report
Data as of: Jun 30, 2015

Next data refresh: Aug 3, 2015

Learning Impact and Value ⬜ ⊠

Respondents in Data Analysis	5
Predicted improvement in performance due to training (adjusted for bias)	31.20%
Projected Benefit to Cost Ratio from Training	15.60

SOURCE: CEB (2016)

Figure 3.5 Instant Insights™ dashboard

Scrap Learning

43%

Benchmark: 27%

@ Help

43%

Benchmark: 27%

Data as of: Mar 12, 2014
Next data refresh: Apr 3, 2014

Potential Savings ⑦

$4,433,437

of estimated potential savings
over the next year.

Scrap Learning
What insights can you leverage to find potential cost savings?

 Support Tools ⑦

Question: The participant materials (manual, presentation handouts, job aids, etc.) will be useful on the job.

Recommendations

Investment

The majority of learning takes place outside of the classroom or elearning environment. Ensure   Medium
that your learning programs provide useful post-training support tools, such as job aids,
performance support tools, communities of practice, and knowledge bases. Emphasize the design
and development of these resources at least as much in your program development process as
the program itself.

Incorporate in your design and development learner needs that go beyond simply learning to do   Medium
something for the first time. Provide resources that address additional needs such as when they
go to apply what they have learned, but may have forgotten some details, as well as when they
need more depth to address a more complex or challenging scenario.

Alignment
This training aligns with the business priorities and goals identified by my organization.

Support Tools
I will be provided adequate resources (time, money, equipment) to successfully apply this training on my job.

Courseware
The scope of the material was appropriate to my needs.

the system automates manual processes (eg survey distribution, data collection, analysis and reporting) and puts information in the hands of end users who can make decisions about how to improve the quality of training.

Conclusion

Technology innovations bring substantial improvements for businesses, typically in the form of process efficiencies. In the information age, business intelligence systems are providing competitive advantage by turning data into information. Learning and development departments benefit from systems and technology as they leverage mobile devices for just-in-time learning, webinars for reaching remote workers, and learning management systems for organizing, deploying and tracking learning events. Technology is also influencing evaluation efforts. Evaluation and testing systems are replacing large evaluation groups. More importantly, these systems are integrating principles of business intelligence tools to transform data into information. Systems help determine whether development programmes are effective, they provide L&D professionals with information to continuously improve courses, and they provide insights that can be shared with executives to assure them that investments in L&D are valuable and should be continued.

Endnotes

1 Everett Rogers (2003) *Diffusion of Innovations*, 5th edn, Free Press, New York, NY.

2 Adapted from Diffusion of Innovation Curves. Graphic copied from Wikipedia page: https://en.wikipedia.org/wiki/Diffusion_of_innovations.

3 7 Gary S Becker, *Human Capital: A theoretical and empirical analysis with special reference to education*, 3rd edn, University of Chicago Press, Chicago, IL.

4 The Royal Swedish Academy of Sciences (1992) Nobel Prize Laureate in economic sciences 1992 [online] http://www.nobelprize.org/nobel_prizes/economic-sciences/laureates/1992/press.html.

5 Peter Wilby (2013) Margaret Thatcher's education legacy is still with us – driven on by Gove, *Guardian*, 15 April [online] http://www.theguardian.com/education/2013/apr/15/margaret-thatcher-education-legacy-gove.

6 Margaret Thatcher, Wikipedia: https://en.wikipedia.org/wiki/Margaret_Thatcher.

8 David L Vance (2010) *The Business of Learning: How to manage corporate training to improve your bottom line*, Poudre River Press, Windsor, CO.

9 Patti Phillips (2012) *The Bottomline on ROI: Benefits and barriers to measuring learning, performance improvement, and human resources programs*, 2nd edn, ROI Institute and HRDQ, pp 39–40.

10 Jack Phillips (1997) *Return on Investment in Training and Performance Improvement Programs: A step-by-step manual for calculating the financial return*, Gulf Publishing Company, Houston, TX.

11 Association for Talent Development (2014) *2014 State of the Industry Report*, ATD.

12 Nick Bontis (2009) The Predictive Learning Impact Model, whitepaper, KnowledgeAdvisors, Chicago, IL.

13 Chris McManus, Nucleus Research (2012) Business analytics applications return $10.66 for every dollar invested, nucleus research analysis finds, Nucleus Research [online] http://nucleusresearch.com/press/analytics-applications-return-10-66-for-every-dollar-invested-nucleus-research-finds/.

14 CEB (2013) The analytics era: transforming HR's impact on the business, CEB [online] https://www.cebglobal.com/shl/images/uploads/linkau13-CLC-The-Analytics-Era.pdf.

15 Hailey Hedge (2015) Skillsoft and IBM research unveil new applications for big data in learning and talent development at the 2015 Global Skillsoft Perspectives customer event, PRWeb [online] http://www.prweb.com/releases/2015/05/prweb12732536.htm.

Access to the CEB resources cited in this book is limited to members. For information about membership, please contact CEB's Member Support Centre at CEB.Support@cebglobal.com or +1-866-913-2632.

Linking learning to business impact

04

What works?

It's a fair question. Anyone who creates talent development programmes asks that question. The answer can be somewhat elusive,
and unfortunately, this chapter will not give you one. However, it *will*
help you use tools that will help you determine what might work for
you. To do so, let's consider an example of a development opportunity and several loosely related yet relevant stories.

Imagine for a moment that Alison, an instructional designer, is
given the opportunity to redesign the sales curriculum for a product
company. She is excited by the chance to create something that will
be new, innovative and most of all effective – that the programme she
designs will improve sales performance and improve the bottom line.
She is also a bit overwhelmed. Her graduate programme did not teach
her which sales curriculum is the most effective for the products in
her industry. But she does know how to apply an instructional design
process, ADDIE,[1] to develop a programme to meet the business needs
of her stakeholders. Alison wishes she could search a library and find
a catalogue of programmes that describes a) the components of an
effective sales programme, b) what would be achieved (eg improved
sales), c) the requirements including costs for resources and materials,
and d) which components contribute most to improved outcomes.
With such information, Alison could select the programme that
would produce the greatest financial impact while also adhering to
budget, design and delivery constraints. Wouldn't it be valuable if
Alison could look behind the marketing materials for Spin Selling,[2]

The Speed of Trust,[3] Solution Selling,[4] or The Challenger Sale[5] to determine what works best?

Sir Ken Robinson, a renowned proponent of education reform, has said, 'Don't be surprised if the systems you design operate as expected.'[6] He is referring to state-funded school systems in particular, and his statement is intended as both a compliment and a criticism. State-funded schools are designed to educate children along a standard curriculum; every child learns the same materials in the same way. They are designed to elevate basic skills across the population including maths, reading, science, music and history among others. Not surprisingly, state-funded schools, on average, work. In the United States the proportion of Americans with a high school diploma is almost 90 per cent – higher now than ever before.[7] The criticism raised by Sir Ken Robinson, even as these goals are realized, is simple. Creativity is lost in the design. His argument continues that a well-educated populace is a more productive populace, but it is also a populace without creativity and potentially lacking innovation. Without innovation, a country (or an organization) cannot evolve and will eventually fail.

Training is an opportunity not only to convey standards for performance, but also to innovate – to try new things and apply new learning. Will the training that Alison creates operate as she expects? Will it bring innovative processes to the sales force? Will it educate the sales force effectively and lead to increased sales and revenue?

Before answering these questions, consider for a moment the Eastman Kodak Company.[8] This camera and film company evolved from the late 19th century, through the 20th century into the early 21st century by applying new technologies for building cameras and creating film. It was a wildly successful company because it innovated. The classic accordion photo box with an exploding phosphorous flash was replaced by a small hand-held stereoscopic camera which eventually gave way to the single-lens reflex (SLR) cameras. Then came accessories like interchangeable zoom and wide-angle lens, automatic flashes and auto-winding film.

Then in one revolutionary moment, the fate of Eastman Kodak changed. Some might argue that competition with Fujifilm brought

Kodak to its knees. Fujifilm certainly cut into profits, but in reality, it was a set of unanticipated competitors that brought Kodak's decline: digital cameras and the iPhone. Digital cameras broke the mould on how images were stored. That was the beginning of the end of film, and then Apple launched the iPhone, a small, wireless phone with a camera built in. The need for film and film processing plummeted. The photo quality from the iPhone was poor compared to professional SLR cameras, but it eliminated the hassle of film – pictures were stored digitally on the phone and could be downloaded and deleted to create a fresh roll. The iPhone also provided a way to share photos in a variety of ways instantaneously through text, e-mail, Facebook and other social media sites. Should Eastman Kodak have innovated and created a phone business? Should it have partnered with Apple or other phone companies to survive? Or was time up for the photo giant? In the blink of an eye – or the click of a shutter – Eastman Kodak's market dominance disappeared.

What do these stories have to do with training and measurement? Innovation is an essential part of training. In the past 20 years, the industry has been transformed by learning management systems, e-learning tools, webinars and the Internet. Companies that continue to innovate will continue to have an advantage. The newest wave of innovation focuses on data – not the collection and storage of it, but processing, analysing and reporting it. In their book *Big Data*, Viktor Mayer-Schonberger and Kenneth Cukier state: 'The real revolution is not in the machines that calculate data but in the data itself and how we use it.'[9] Data provides information and information provides insight. The organizations that can leverage business intelligence systems that process data and provide information for decision making will gain competitive advantage.

In October 2012, *Harvard Business Review* shone a spotlight on this message when they dedicated the entire issue to Big Data.[10] Various articles explained that organizations have an abundance of data about how they operate, what customers buy and how they feel. These data sets require special tools for analysis as well as a special type of employee, a data scientist, to analyse them. According to the articles, data scientists will be responsible for mining data and providing insights. Learning and development departments are part of this same data-rich business environment, and L&D data provides insight into which aspects of talent development work.

So we return to Alison and her need to build effective training. In order for her to know what works, she first has to answer the question, *why* does training work?

Why does it work?

Why? It's a simple question. But at the heart of it is a complex issue – cause and effect. When a child asks, 'Why does the sun rise?' a parent can explain the physics behind the solar system, gravitational fields and orbiting planets. Physics is an exact science with immutable laws. When a CEO asks, 'Is the new sales training working?' an L&D manager may provide a solid answer such as 'Yes, our attendees are learning the new process and 95 per cent are applying it on the job. We are seeing a 5 per cent rise in sales this quarter and 15 per cent of that rise is due to training.' That answer is far from immutable, but it does rely on best practices for evaluating talent development programmes, which employ substantial rigour but are far less exact and far more mutable than the laws of physics.

The beauty of the human animal is that it has free will. The reason for doing X may be motivated by Y on Monday and motivated by Z on Tuesday. Cause and effect are difficult to assess among people. The disciplines of anthropology, sociology and psychology apply scientific principles to investigate human activities, but free will acts like a trump card when trying to establish laws of human behaviour. At best, scientists in these fields can state, 'Usually, people do this', or 'Often we observe', or 'People tend to behave in this way in this situation'. Despite the large variation in human behaviours, scientists still strive to uncover cause-and-effect relationships.

One simple way to begin considering cause and effect is to create a logic model. Simply put, a logic model is a graphic view of the expected relationship between a set of inputs and outcomes. If a sales training programme is implemented, what are the expected outcomes? The W K Kellogg Foundation describes how to create a logic model graphic, which is a detailed visual representation of the logical connection between inputs and outputs.[11] An example of the main components of the logic model is shown in Figure 4.1.

Figure 4.1 Simple logic model

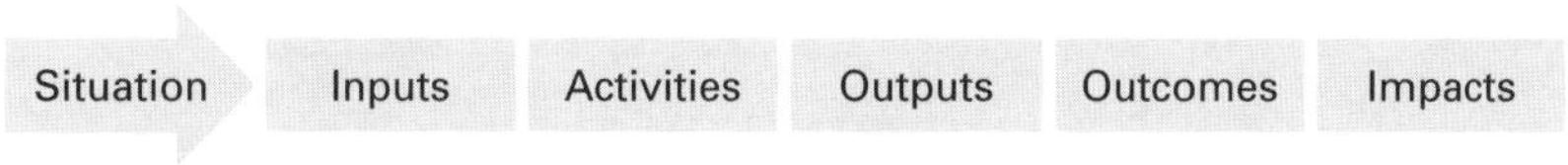

Situation	Inputs	Activities	Outputs	Outcomes	Impacts

SOURCE: W K Kellogg Foundation (2006)

Figure 4.2 shows the logic model for a sales training programme. Notice that the components of the logic model at the top have been modified to be more relevant to a talent development programme. It is valuable to create a logic model for any strategic, visible or costly programme that is going to be evaluated in depth because the model articulates the connections between the resources that are input into training, the simple outcomes (eg trained professionals), the expected short-term and long-term behavioural changes and the benefits to the organization. The logic model should be shared with stakeholders to get their feedback and confirm that the model is rational. It can also uncover irrational thoughts. A programme that instructs auditors how to hang-glide in order to become better auditors is not logically sound because there is no apparent connection between hang-gliding and auditing. A review by the stakeholders also provides an opportunity to quantify the expected outcomes. A stakeholder who expects a doubling of sales revenue due to a new training programme may be too optimistic.

A simple logic model is not sufficient. While it documents and simplifies the suspected causal pathway, it does not exercise sufficient scientific rigour to establish causation. In theory, it is a good start, but more is needed.

Figure 4.2 Logic model for a sales programme

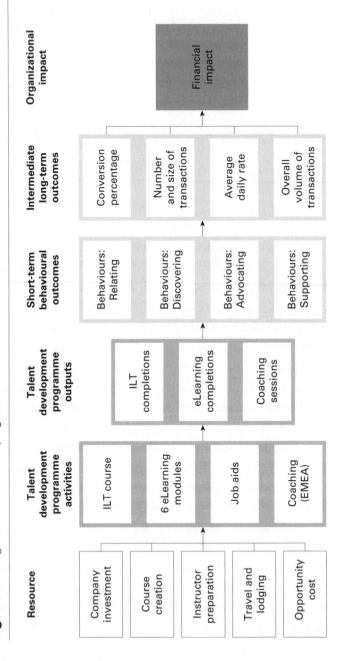

Establishing cause and effect with humans is a challenging task, but not impossible. To determine whether talent development programmes work, and what aspects work best, we need to follow some scientific tenets that help us assess cause and effect.[12]

- **Temporal precedence**

  In order to show that A caused B, A must happen in time before B. If performance improvement is the desired outcome of development programmes, then those programmes must come first. If performance improves before those programmes, the improvement is likely due to other factors such as practice, experience, coaching or other influencers.

- **Covariation of cause and effect**

  When analysing data for impact, covariation is essential. That is, if a treatment like a talent development programme is applied, then the outcome measure like performance must change. With X treatment, Y performance improves. It is also essential to show covariation when the treatment is not present. Without X treatment, Y performance does not improve or declines. If performance improves with *and* without X treatment, there is no covariation with training and no causation.

- **Eliminating alternative explanations**

  The hardest part of demonstrating causation is controlling all the other factors that could influence the outcome. There are many plausible factors that could improve performance as much as or more than development programmes, including individual experience, coaching, new processes, new tools, market forces, realignment of goals, incentives, lack of competition and many, many others. Measuring and controlling all of these variables are a daunting, if not impossible, task. This is the greatest challenge when determining causation, and we will address this next in the section covering experimental designs.

So how do we determine cause and effect with talent development programmes? Let's address the three requisites using a sales development programme. Assume for a moment that sales are flat for a random group of sales professionals. They attend a sales course and slowly their sales metrics begin to rise over six months. In this situation, we've addressed temporal precedence – *after* the course, sales went up. We have also established part of covariation. With training, sales go up. We cannot assess whether sales go down if we remove the knowledge and skills transferred during the programme because we cannot remove them, nor can we determine whether other factors can explain the results. It is entirely possible that sales would have risen without the course because of customer buying patterns (eg Black Friday and the pre-Christmas rush), experience or many other factors. We need a more effective way of assessing covariation that also eliminates alternative explanations. A more rigorous approach is necessary.

Experimental designs

The single best approach to determine causality is to employ an experimental design.[13] An experimental design is 'a plan for assigning experimental units to treatment conditions'.[14] It is also known as a time-motion study, a control-group experiment and a clinical trials design. A design is required when an experiment is employed to determine if a treatment (eg a talent development programme) has a desired outcome. Four things must be managed: group conditions, measurement, equal treatment and randomization:

- **Group conditions**
  There must be at least two groups: an experimental group that receives the treatment (in this case a development programme) and a second group that does not. It is advisable but not necessary to include a placebo group, meaning a group that receives a programme that is unrelated to the core development course for the experimental group. In pharmaceutical studies, the dosage of a treatment is also varied. In the L&D world, a dosage could be the total hours of development provided on a topic, or additional learning components like job aids, role play, or coaching.

- **Measurement**
  The critical measures for the study (eg sales metrics) must be tracked for the experimental group and the control group – and any

additional groups included in the study. Moreover, the measures should be tracked before the development programme and after it. If there are concerns about seasonality (eg cyclical buying), then a full cycle of data should be collected before and after the programme. Typically, this means a year of data before and after. The unit of analysis is also important. The results will eventually be compared at the group level, but it is ideal to collect the data for each individual in the study and then aggregate results within groups. From a statistical perspective, the power to find statistically significant results increases as the number of people and the number of data points increases.

- **Equal treatment**

  If the impact of training is going to be assessed, each group in the design must be treated equally. This means that no additional factors should be applied to help the experimental group or hinder all other groups. If the experimental group gets the programme and coaching, then the placebo groups should get a different programme and coaching. The control group gets nothing. In the end, the leaders of the study should be able to say, 'All other things being equal...' or 'The only factor that was different among groups was training.'

- **Randomization**

  This is the key aspect of an experimental design which adds scientific rigour. Randomization means to randomly assign participants to each of the conditions. If there are 100 participants and two groups (eg experimental and control), then 50 are assigned to each group, randomly. If there are four groups, then 25 are assigned to each group, randomly. There are many ways to execute random assignment. A common approach is to list the names of participants alphabetically in a spreadsheet like MS Excel and then use a random number generator to assign a random number to each participant. The list can be resorted by the random number and the top half becomes the experimental group and the bottom half the control group. Or even numbers become the experimental group and odd numbers become the control group. There are many ways to randomly assign people to conditions and those protocols can be found on the Internet with ease. Regardless of the method, randomization is essential.

An additional step. Even when scientists apply experimental designs as prescribed they can sometimes find misleading results – Type 1 (false positive results) and Type 2 (false negative results) errors. To increase confidence in the cause-and-effect results, it is recommended to run more than one trial. This could consist of multiple experimental and control groups simultaneously or multiple trials in sequence.

Why is randomization essential for an experimental design? Consider the last of the three requirements for determining cause and effect – alternative explanations. There are many factors that could influence the alternative causes for the results that are observed. A good researcher might be able to measure and control statistically for influencers like seasonality or experience or geography, but it is impossible to control for *all* such influencers. Random assignment levels the playing field. If there is a characteristic among the participants that influences the outcome and it is resident in half of the group, randomization ensures there is an equal chance that the characteristic will appear in the experimental group and the control group when participants are assigned. In this way, randomization makes each group in the experiment equal before the study begins. If all characteristics of the groups are equal, and they are treated equally – except for the experimental programme – the results at the end of the study are most likely due to the influence of treatment.

Figure 4.3 provides a graphical depiction of an experimental design. Notably, multiple conditions are shown including condition A, condition B, a placebo and a control group. The results that are gathered during an experimental design allow investigators to determine conclusively whether the intervention (eg a talent development programme) has an influence on outcome measures.

Here is an important point on terminology. When a group is randomly assigned to a non-treatment condition, it is called a control group. If it is not randomly assigned, it is called a comparison group. Comparison groups will be discussed in the next section on alternatives to experimental designs.

While experimental designs are the most rigorous designs and arguably the best approach for determining causality, there are several drawbacks. They are costly to implement because they may take upwards of a year or longer to complete. They require dedicated resources to implement and manage which translates to effort and

Figure 4.3 Example of an experimental design

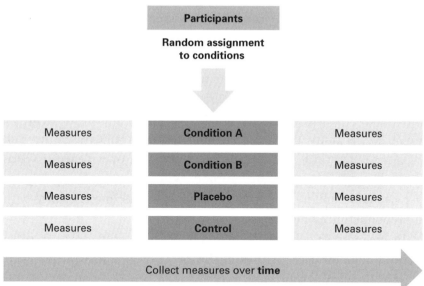

cost. They are difficult to execute because they require business outcomes data (eg sales metrics) that has to be extracted from an organization's business systems. Randomization is theoretically easy, but practically difficult to implement. Without explicit protocols or standard operating procedures, HR and L&D professionals have difficulty executing steps to accurately assign participants to conditions. The value for implementing an experimental design is substantial, but the results take time to manifest and require vast human and financial resources.

Reality check. You may be asking yourself 'Really? Does it take *that* much effort to really determine cause and effect?' Well, the answer is 'Yes'. However, there are alternatives and we will discuss them here.

Alternatives to experimental designs

If experimental designs are so hard to implement, what alternatives are available? Many designs are available, and several will be described here. The critical issue is randomization. When randomization is not employed, it is highly unlikely that the experimental and comparison groups are equal. As such, it is impossible to eliminate *all* alternative explanations. Without such rigour, the results should not be considered conclusive. A causal relationship may be likely, but it is not fully confirmed.

At this point, it may be valuable to consider the legal system and how it views evidence. For extremely important criminal cases, such as capital murder, the jury must determine guilt 'beyond a reasonable doubt'. Based on the evidence, they must be certain that the defendant is guilty. For lesser criminal cases or civil cases, a jury can deliver a guilty verdict based on a 'preponderance of evidence'. Experimental designs demonstrate causality with evidence that is beyond a reasonable doubt. Alternative designs demonstrate causality with a preponderance of evidence.

In business environments, a preponderance of evidence is often good enough for decision making. Leaders may not have the patience, staff or financial resources to implement an experimental design. For this reason, it is valuable to examine a variety of alternative designs that contribute evidence of causality for decision making.

Alternative designs

The following designs are presented from weakest to strongest:

- **After only**
  This design gathers results only after the development programme has been deployed. No information is gathered before or during the programme and no comparison group is used. Most programmes deploy this approach and administer a Level 1 evaluation after the programme is finished. This design provides a limited amount of information. It is weak because it cannot show temporal impact (eg performance could have been equally strong before the programme), covariance (there are no points of comparison), nor can it eliminate alternative explanations.

- **After only with a comparison group**
  This design gathers data after the development programme is deployed, usually with a Level 1 evaluation. It cannot demonstrate

temporal impact, but it can begin to show covariation. If the metrics for the programme group improve while the metrics for the comparison group stay the same, there is some evidence that the programme leads to improvement. Alternative explanations have not been ruled out.

- **Quasi-experimental design**
  This design replicates the approach of an experimental design with an experimental group (eg development programme) and at least one comparison group. A quasi-experimental design looks identical to the experimental design shown in Figure 4.3 except that participants are not randomly assigned to conditions. Temporal order and covariation are controlled with this approach, but threats to alternative explanations are not ruled out.

- **A-B-A**
  This design is used when only one group, the group receiving the development programme, can be observed. This happens frequently within organizations. For example, auditing firms train every new hire. If they did not train every new hire, the firm would be exposed to risk. As such, the use of a non-training control group is not possible. They would not expose themselves to risk by training only half of the new hires for the sake of experimenting with the effectiveness of a programme. In the A-B-A design, the first of the three phases of the design is the baseline phase, 'A'. During this phase, performance metrics are gathered before the programme is implemented. The second phase, 'B', is when the programme is applied. Again, performance measures are tracked over time. During this phase, measures are expected to improve. The third phase, 'A', is a return to baseline. The treatment is withdrawn. For development programmes, this design is not practical because it is difficult or impossible to withdraw it. The knowledge and skills that have been gained during the programme cannot be removed. This design works better with support tools like job aids or technology tools that enhance performance on the job – something that can be truly removed during the third phase. This approach addresses temporal impact and covariance, but it does not control for alternative explanations.

Here are some simple improvements to these designs that will provide more valuable evidence of causation:

- **Use SmartSheets**

  Since Don Kirkpatrick's Four Levels of Evaluation were published, organizations have deployed Level 1 evaluations after training to gauge learner satisfaction. A common term for these surveys is 'Smile Sheets'. This comes from the use of smiley and frowny face icons above the Likert scale. Likert scales are numeric scales placed beside a survey question. The scale displays a set of points (usually five or seven) that are labelled with numbers (1–5 or 1–7 and labels like 'Strongly disagree' to 'Strongly agree'); the numeric and semantic labels convey a continuum with equal intervals. When survey respondents cannot read (eg children or people who are not familiar with the language on the survey), icons such as smiley faces are often used. Rather than Smile Sheets, CEB recommends using SmartSheets to gather feedback. SmartSheets include questions from all four levels of Kirkpatrick's model and estimates of Return on Investment. The value of SmartSheets is that they provide insight on multiple levels. First, they provide information about satisfaction with content, instructors, environment and materials (L1) and learning (L2). Looking back on the event at the end of training, learners provide valid and reliable ratings of their experience. SmartSheets also provide predictive information. Learners indicate whether they *will* apply what they learned, whether training *will* improve individual performance and whether training *will* improve business performance. Studies show these measures are valid and reliable.[15] These measures become leading indicators of success which correlate with actual knowledge gain scores, individual performance and organizational performance. The value for learning and business leaders is simple: these measures provide timely information for decision making.

- **Confirmatory measures**

  As with the A-B-A design, repeated measures designs help determine performance over time and covariation. Using the right tools, they can also increase validity by providing confirmatory information.

With repeated measures designs, the first measure usually comes right after the development programme is deployed. Again, one should gather predictive information about Levels 3–5 (eg I will apply learning; learning will improve my performance; learning will have a positive ROI). The second measure, a follow-up survey, gathers feedback 60–90 days after the programme, allowing learners ample opportunity to apply what they learned back on the job. Questions on the follow-up survey align with the initial survey, but rather than asking 'Will you apply?' the follow-up survey asks for confirmatory information with questions like 'How much did you apply?' and 'How much did your performance improve?' A third level of confirmatory information is gathered for some courses – those that are considered strategic, visible and costly. A survey is sent to the managers of learners. Questions are similar to those asked on the follow-up survey sent to learners, and managers provide feedback about the learners: 'Have they applied training?' 'Has their performance improved?' 'Has training helped improve business performance?'

- **Use benchmarks for comparison**
  A comparison group is not always available for an experimental, quasi-experimental or even an A-B-A design. However, comparison information can be sought from benchmarks. If an organization uses the same questions on its survey forms (eg post-event, follow-up and manager follow-up), it can aggregate results for each question across courses. In this way, the average score across courses creates a benchmark for each question. Depending on the layers within the organization, the benchmark can be aggregated at the course level (eg same course with multiple class deployments), the curriculum level, the business unit level or the organizational level. Benchmarks provide a point of reference. If a course is substantially underperforming a benchmark, it is worthwhile to determine why by looking at the evaluation results so improvements can be made. If a course is substantially outperforming a benchmark, it is worth investigating to determine what factors make it successful and should be replicated in future courses.

One last design is worth sharing, and it combines design and statistics:

- **Causal modelling**

  A causal model is a theoretical model that graphically and statistically describes the relationships among concepts. Within the realm of learning and development, the concepts are the factors that make development programmes effective. If we consider Kirkpatrick's model for a moment, we could create a causal model that tests the relationships among the Four Levels of Evaluation. The model might hypothesize: if learners are satisfied (L1), they will learn (L2), and they will apply what they learn (L3), which will improve their own performance and organizational performance (L4). This is a simple linear model. Other models are not so simple. For example, what are the contributors to heart disease? There are many: genetic factors, weight, age, stress, diet and many others. If we were to create an accurate model using these factors to predict a heart attack, the model would not be linear. There would be relationships among many of the variables. The input from multiple variables would create the best predictive model for determining the conditions when a heart attack would likely occur. Causal modelling uses logic to create a reasonable chain of causation among variables and then applies advanced statistical analysis to a data set related to those variables to test which pathways are the strongest and what factors are the best predictors.

  In 2009, Nick Bontis, a professor at McMaster University in Canada, examined evaluation data from the Metrics That Matter™ system which included more than 70 clients and almost half a million data points. Together with the input from measurement experts at KnowledgeAdvisors (now CEB Metrics That Matter™), Bontis created and tested a model to determine which factors contribute most to learning and whether learning leads to improvement in individual and business performance. His analysis produced the Predictive Learning Impact Model that is shown in Figure 4.4.[16] The model shows that there are three factors that drive learning: instructor effectiveness, courseware quality (eg quality of materials and delivery in class) and worthwhile investment (eg learners' belief that training was worthwhile). Of these factors, worthwhile investment is the strongest predictor of learning. If all of these factors are performing well during a course, learning will be optimized. If learning is optimized, then learners intend to apply it. This leads to actual application at 60 days and business improvement at 60 days. The causal pathway can be found by tracking the arrows with the highest values.

This approach is termed causal modelling, but causation is fully dependent upon having an exhaustive data set. That is, it assumes that every meaningful and influential factor is measured and that large volumes of data are included in the analysis. Among our three criteria for determining causal relationships, this approach accounts for temporal order and most certainly accounts for covariation. Well-specified causal models should account for all influential variables or they will suffer from an omitted variable bias. Understandably, not all models can reach this level of comprehensiveness but administrators of such models should try hard to get as close as possible.

A note on statistical analysis. Statistical analysis is a mathematical tool used to determine group differences (eg are the scores for one course significantly higher or lower than another?) and relationships (eg as scrap learning is reduced, does performance improve?). They do not determine causation. A design, not statistics, allows us to draw conclusions about causality. When used with the right design, statistics help determine whether training has a significant effect – a change in performance that is probably not due to chance. Logic *and* statistics are needed to assess causality.

Sometimes results appear to show a relationship but the statistical test of significance fails, creating a false negative – a relationship exists but there is not enough statistical power to detect the difference. Researchers refer to this as a substantive relationship (or a substantive difference when comparing group differences). Consider the definition of learning analytics we shared at the beginning of Chapter 2. This is where the 'art' of analysis comes into play. There always needs to be a layer of interpretation on whether the size of the impact of the development programme is large enough. In this situation, it is essential to consult the statistical analysts, the design team and the stakeholders to determine if the outcomes are meaningful and if the programme should continue.

Figure 4.4 The Predictive Learning Impact Model

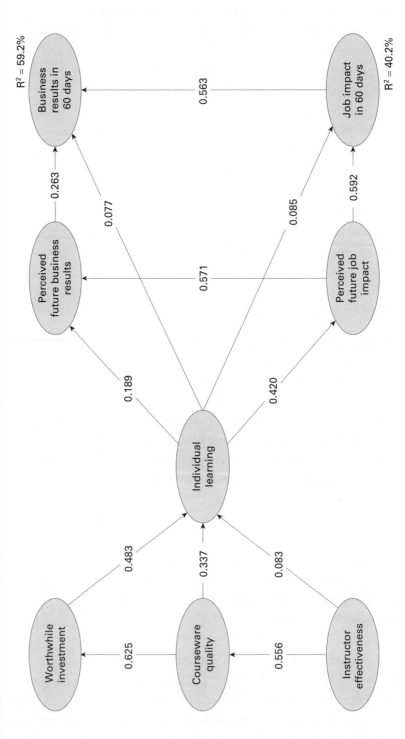

SOURCE: Bontis (2009)

The end of the null hypothesis – almost

One of the critical steps in determining causation is formulating hypotheses. The most common hypothesis for learning analytics is this: talent development programmes improve performance. When conducting research, the scientific approach cannot *prove* a relationship between the programme and performance improvement. However, the approach can disprove that there is no relationship. The difference can be a bit confusing. When crafting a hypothesis to test, the appropriate approach is to create a null hypothesis, meaning a hypothesis which states there is no relationship between training and performance. If we find that there is a relationship among the data, we reject the null hypothesis. For example, with our sales programme, our null hypothesis is that sales training has no effect on sales. Let's assume we can implement a randomized experimental design. When the results show that the programme group and the non-programme control group have roughly equal metrics both before and after training, we cannot reject the null hypothesis. We accept it; there are no differences between the two groups. Training had no effect. On the other hand, if the results show no difference between groups before the programme and a significantly higher set of sales metrics for the programme group compared to the non-programme group after training, we reject the null (eg that the two groups are equal) and claim that the change in sales metrics is most likely caused by the training programme.

Null hypothesis testing goes hand in hand with experimental and quasi-experimental designs. And for this reason, it is difficult, time consuming and expensive to test one hypothesis at a time. Rogers boldly stated in 2010 that null hypothesis testing will become less and less prevalent.[17] Certainly, it will still be necessary for some critical experiments, like clinical trials for drugs. Yet, there are several forces that are converging that will marginalize null hypothesis testing. First, the big data movement makes it clear that we currently have massive data sets – some too big to analyse – and we expect more, not less, to come. Second, business operates at the speed of data, not the speed of null hypothesis testing. Third, in-system analytics tools make rapid analysis possible. Leaders need to know what is the best way forward given the available data right now – not the most rigorous data next year. In *Big Data*, Schonberger and Cukier emphasize that the data sets are massive enough to represent the entire population in real time and that simple analytics, like correlation, are sufficient to bring valuable and timely insight. Correlation does not equal causation, but Schonberger and Cukier emphasize that answers to *what*, not *why*, are often good enough for decision making.

At this time, null hypothesis testing continues to be the most powerful approach in many situations. However, methods like causal modelling and real-time analytics should be considered when experimental designs are difficult or impossible to apply.

BUSINESS IMPACT CASE STUDY
Hilton Worldwide University

The remainder of this chapter describes a case study from Hilton Worldwide University (HWU). A quasi-experimental design was used to determine the effectiveness of a commercial programme for revenue managers within hotels called Revenue Management at Work. HWU partnered with CEB to employ a design that included a retrospective and prospective approach for gathering data using survey tools to *estimate* performance improvement and actual revenue data to *determine* the financial impact of the programme. The programme took nearly a full year to complete – a reasonable time frame for an impact study. Our efforts produced a preponderance of evidence that the programme is having its desired impact on behaviours (eg adjusting room prices to reflect market demands) and consequently revenue increases for the hotels.

The impact study was implemented using a five-step process:

- develop a logic model;

- create an analytics and reporting strategy;

- design and develop data collection instruments;

- deploy instruments to collect data;

- analyse and report results.

The logic model shown earlier in Figure 4.2 provides a basic outline for a programme like Revenue Management at Work. It describes resources that go into the development of a programme, including the financial investment, course materials, instructor preparation, travel and even the opportunity cost of taking revenue management professionals out of the field and setting them in training. The development activities are also described, such as the multi-day, instructor-led course with tools and templates to facilitate analysis, a network of other managers, and coaching from supervisors.

The assumption in the logic model is that the development efforts will lead to short-term and long-term performance improvement. The short-term improvements align to the key behavioural components of the programme: negotiated rates, competitive pricing, extended stay pricing, monitoring performance against in-market competitors, etc. The long-term outcomes are critical business measures called Revenue Per Available Room (RevPAR), index per cent change (RPI%) and Revenue Per Available Room Index Impact (RevPAR Index Impact). These measures are composite scores which compare each hotel's performance against the performance of competitive hotels in the local market. Data is available monthly. If the programme improves short- and long-term performance for attendees compared to the performance of non-attendees, then the organization will benefit with higher sales and greater revenue and market share.

As a second step in the process, the CEB team collaborated with the HWU team to determine what analysis and reports were needed for the programme. Reporting proved quite simple. The project team wanted to see timely reports of the survey results as they were collected. This provided a way to monitor the ongoing quality of the programme. The reports went directly to the programme manager who also shared with his director. The final report was the most important summary document, and it consisted of an MS PowerPoint file which documented the programme and how it helped improve individual and organizational performance. The project team provided a detailed version for the programme manager and a simplified version with high-level impact statements for HWU leaders and business leaders. The analysis and reporting process outlined the number and types of reports, report content, audience and timing of the reporting process.

The CEB team and the HWU team also collaborated to create the survey instruments used to collect data. The instruments targeted the learners three times: immediately after training, six months later and 12 months later. Surveys asked if the learners had applied the specific behaviours learned in the programme, whether the programme had improved their performance and whether it was helping the organization achieve business goals.

Table 4.1 shows feedback provided by the follow-up surveys with a comparison to benchmarks. The data were collected on a five-point Likert scale (1 = strongly disagree and 5 = strongly agree) and the percentages in the table represent the top two boxes (eg the top two box value equals the sum of the percentage of respondents selecting 4 or 5).

Table 4.1 Transfer of knowledge and skills

Measure	6 months	12 months	Benchmark
Training improved my job performance.	83%	80%	55%
How critical was applying the content of the training to your job success?	80%	87%	62%
Applied learning within six weeks	94%	100%	90%

Learners were also asked to rate if they are now able (or now *better* able) to apply their skills because of the revenue management programme. Among the 16 specific components of the programme, 13 received average ratings of 4.00 or higher on the five-point agreement scale, indicating the course successfully addressed the vast majority of critical behaviours for the job. The results in Table 4.1 and the strong behavioural ratings just mentioned are leading indicators of the successful transfer of knowledge and skills from the programme to the work place. They are also leading indicators of business outcomes such as revenue per available room, RPI% and RevPAR index impact.

In order to estimate how much training improved performance, the surveys collected data using three questions that align to the Phillips' ROI Methodology.[18] Those questions ask the learners to estimate three things:

1 How much do they expect their performance will improve related to the content of the course due to all factors including the development programme?

2 How much of that improvement is due to the development programme only?

3 How much work time is actually spent on tasks related to the development programme?

On the follow-up evaluation, learners reflect on what they have actually applied and how much their performance has improved when they provide ratings. The percentage values from each question are multiplied together. This value is then adjusted downward by 35 per cent to account for response bias and overestimation. The process is called 'estimation, isolation, isolation and adjustment'. Figure 4.5 shows the average values from the learner evaluations for the revenue management programme. The computed value is the estimated performance improvement due to training; this value is 18 per cent, which is almost twice the value of the benchmark (9 per cent) for the travel and leisure industry. Looking back to the logic model (Figure 4.2), this measure and all others shown in Table 4.1 comprise many of the short-term measures of programme impact.

Figure 4.5 Estimated performance improvement due to a development programme

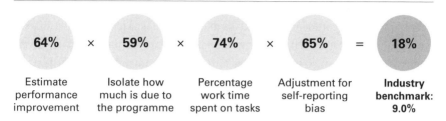

| **64%** | × | **59%** | × | **74%** | × | **65%** | = | **18%** |
| Estimate performance improvement | | Isolate how much is due to the programme | | Percentage work time spent on tasks | | Adjustment for self-reporting bias | | **Industry benchmark: 9.0%** |

It is important to note for this project that the evaluation team made a slight modification to the process. Instead of the using question 3, which focuses on work time, the team chose to use a question about how much learning was actually applied. The team thought the application question was a reasonable surrogate of work time and used it. The items are well correlated in the MTM system. The equation in Figure 4.5 is labelled according to the prescribed methodology using 'percentage work time spent on tasks' for the third question, though this value for Hilton came from the application question.

This value, 18 per cent, can be used as a conservative estimate of the influence of the development programme on revenue management figures. In the absence of any other information, Hilton could estimate that the performance of its trained revenue management team would improve by this amount. If the trained revenue management team generated $1,000,000 in revenue last year, Hilton can expect that this same group would generate $1,180,000 ($1M × 18% + $1M = $1.18M) after attending training.

From a methodological perspective, the results so far were collected using an after-only design. This approach does address temporal precedence; the programme comes before the collection of measures about performance, but the design does not address well the other two criteria for determining causation. There is some covariation; performance improves 18 per cent for the programme group. However, we do not see the other side of covariation. Without the programme, does performance stay flat or decline? Lastly, this design does not address alternative explanations for these results. The estimated improvement due to the programme (18 per cent) could be caused by coaching, market forces, improved sales processes, incentives or countless other factors – although we have asked learners to estimate only the impact of the programme, so we can be fairly certain that most other factors are ruled out. In this way, we are gathering a preponderance of evidence, not evidence beyond a shadow of doubt.

In order to increase the rigour of the design, the MTM and HWU teams collaborated to identify a comparison group and gather the same set of business measures for both the programme attendees and the comparison group. The comparison group was matched based on the hotel and whether the revenue manager at the hotel had attended the Revenue Management at Work programme. One hundred and fifty-six hotels with attendees were matched against other hotels in the Hilton portfolio of brands. The matching process focused on the market location (eg Nashville, TN), the hotel brand (eg Hilton Garden Inn or Embassy Suites, etc), the hotel size (eg number of rooms) and a handful of other factors. Of the 156 hotels, 65 were matched by brand but were not aligned to the same geographic market. Four were matched to the market but not the brand. In the end, 87 hotels were considered exact matches by market, brand and size. In total the revenue metrics for 174 hotels were tracked: 87 had managers who attended the Revenue Management at Work programme and 87 did not.

The revenue management programme was delivered on a rolling basis starting in January of 2012. Business metrics were collected for 12 months prior to the first event (eg starting in January of 2011) through the end-of-study date which was July 2013. Because training dates varied, not every individual had data for 12 months before and after training. Thus, depending on availability, as much data as possible was gathered. This design allowed the project team to investigate covariation and begin to eliminate alternative explanations like seasonality.

As an example of an outcome measure, Figure 4.6 shows the results of the monthly analysis comparing hotels with attendees and those without. The CEB and HWU team agreed that impact could be expected three months after attending the programme. Near the middle of the graph, the black line for attendees begins to rise and sustains a positive position above the non-attendee line for a full year.

Figure 4.6 Revenue per available room index impact comparison

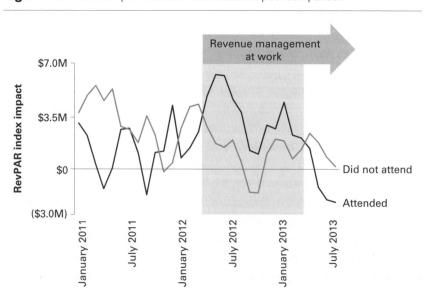

Table 4.2 Financial impact of the revenue management at work programme

Benefits and costs	6 months	12 months
Financial difference between the attendee and non-attendee hotels	$20.0M	$10.9M
Estimated financial impact of training (18%)	$3.7M	$2.0M
Expected market share shift per hotel over 6 or 12 months (divide by 87 hotels)	$42,000	$23,112
Cost of learning per participant	$2,000 / person	$2,000 / person
Payback period	< 2 weeks	> 1 month
ROI ((Benefits – Costs) / Costs)	20.0	10.6

Prior to training, the comparison group is clearly outperforming the attendees. During the first six months after the programme started rolling out, the attendee group shows a dramatic uplift which remains higher than the comparison group for 12 months. After 12 months, performance begins to decline. These results provide evidence of covariation. The onset of the programme covaries with performance improvement and the programme seems to have a limited influential range of 12 months.

Can all of the shift in market share and revenue be attributed to the Revenue Management at Work programme? No, and it should not be. Many factors other than the programme positively and negatively influence this outcome. How much is due to the programme? Based on the evaluation results we collected from learners, they believe their performance improved by 18 per cent due to training. As such, 18 per cent of $20 million equals $3.7 million. This is a conservative estimate of the influence of the programme on market share growth. Table 4.2 summarizes the financial influence of the programme at six months and 12 months. The ROI for the programme at six months is $20:1 and $10.6:1 at 12 months.

From a methodological perspective, this approach – a quasi-experimental design that utilizes a comparison group, multiple revenue measures and repeated measures before and after training – improves the rigour of the study. It does not eliminate alternative explanations for the results, but it does provide a preponderance of evidence that the programme has a substantial positive influence on the revenue performance at hotels with trained employees. When shared with business leaders, the reaction was positive and they decided to continue investing in this programme.

Conclusion

Learning and business leaders want to know whether investments in training are having the desired impact. Are programmes transferring critical knowledge and skills that will improve individual performance and business performance? In order to answer these questions, learning professionals must answer the question, 'Why?' Why does training work? The only way to determine 'Why?' is to examine the cause-and-effect relationships between learning programmes and performance. This chapter emphasized that the most powerful way to establish cause and effect with high confidence, or beyond a reasonable doubt, is to use an experimental design. However, it is often difficult or impossible to randomly assign participants to training and control groups, so alternative designs are necessary. When using alternative designs, cause and effect cannot be determined with certainty, but a preponderance of evidence can be generated. Additionally, even less rigorous designs, such as the after-only approach, provide useful insights in a timely manner that correlate with more expensive and time-consuming approaches like experimental and quasi-experimental designs. In turn, decision makers can have confidence in the results and make well-informed decisions about their learning and development investments and strategies.

In order to meet the information needs of the C-suite, a compromise is required. Most leaders are unwilling to invest the resources required to conduct experimental designs. Such rigorous approaches are also time consuming and do not allow leaders to make timely decisions. Figure 4.7 represents the interplay between scientific rigour associated with the evaluation designs and the amount of effort required to execute them. The sweet spot near the middle represents the needs of business leaders. They want as much rigour and speed as possible while controlling efforts. Throughout the rest of this book, we will share ways to provide timely insights with substantial rigour.

Figure 4.7 The C-suite sweet spot for rigour and effort

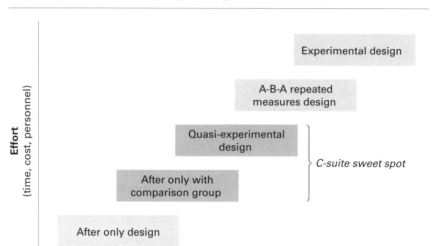

Endnotes

1 Gary R Morrison (2010) *Designing Effective Instruction*, 6th edn, John Wiley, San Francisco, CA.

2 Neil Rackham (1988) *Spin Selling*, McGraw-Hill, New York, NY.

3 Stephen M R Covey and Stephen Covey (2006) *The Speed of Trust: The one thing that changes everything*, Simon & Schuster, New York.

4 Keith M Eades (2003) *The New Solution Selling: The revolutionary sales process that is changing the way people sell*, McGraw-Hill, New York, NY.

5 Matthew Dixon and Brent Adamson (2011) *The Challenger Sale: Taking control of the customer conversation*, Penguin, New York.

6 Ken Robinson (2015) Bring On Learning Innovation, keynote presentation, Skillsoft Perspectives Conference 2015, Orlando, FL.

7 Camille Ryan and Julie Siebens (February 2012) Educational attainment in the US 2009: population characteristics, US Department of Commerce, Economics and Statistics Administration, US Census Bureau [online] http://www.census.gov/prod/2012pubs/p20-566.pdf.

8 Eastman Kodak Company, Wikipedia [online] https://en.wikipedia.org/wiki/Eastman_Kodak.

9 Viktor Mayer-Schonberger and Kenneth Cukier (2013) *Big Data: A revolution that will transform how we live, work, and think*, Houghton Mifflin Harcourt, New York, p 7.

10 *Harvard Business Review* (2012) Getting Control of Big Data (special issue, October).

11 W K Kellogg Foundation (2006) W K Kellogg Foundation Logic Model Guide [online] https://www.wkkf.org/resource-directory/resource/2006/02/wk-kellogg-foundation-logic-model-development-guide.

12 Establishing cause and effect, Social Research Methods [online] http://www.socialresearchmethods.net/kb/causeeff.php.

13 William Shadish, Thomas Cook and Donald Campbell (2001) *Experimental and Quasi-Experimental Designs for Generalized Causal Inference*, 2nd edn, Houghton Mifflin, Boston.

14 Definition of experimental design, Stat Trek [online] http://stattrek.com/experiments/experimental-design.aspx?Tutorial=AP.

15 CEB (2015) CEB Metrics That Matter™ SmartSheets, whitepaper [online] https://www.cebglobal.com/talent-management/metrics-that-matter/resources.html.

16 Nick Bontis (2009) The Predictive Learning Impact Model, whitepaper, KnowledgeAdvisors, Chicago, IL.

17 Joseph Lee Rogers (2010) The epistemology of mathematical and statistical modeling: a quiet methodological revolution, *American Psychologist*, **65** (1), pp 1–12.

18 ROI Institute (2013) The ROI methodology: a brief overview, ROI At-A-Glance Series 2013–02 [online] http://roiinstitute.net/wp-content/uploads/2014/03/The-ROI-Methodology.pdf.

Access to the CEB resources cited in this book is limited to members. For information about membership, please contact CEB's Member Support Centre at CEB.Support@cebglobal.com or +1-866-913-2632.

Scrap learning: the new leading indicator of success

05

Your training programmes are not as good as you think they are

Since its publication in 1975, the ADDIE model[1] has been used to substantially improve the design and development of high-quality courses. At the same time, advances in technology tools have helped solve problems such as reaching a globally distributed workforce, storing course materials, tracking compliance with regulatory training and creating more interactive, skills-based learning events. Learning management systems (LMS) provide efficient and capable storage and delivery platforms. The Internet makes distribution of self-paced, web-based training accessible 24/7, interactive platforms facilitate virtual instructor-led events, and social media applications enable peer-to-peer learning. Gamification is taking online learning to new levels of interactivity with challenging and entertaining applications. Testing systems are even available to send exam questions at random intervals to mobile devices to test and reinforce knowledge and skill acquisition.

Despite these improvements in the proliferation, reach and quality of development programmes, corporate leaders still question the value of data related to their people investments. In 2012, PwC gathered opinions from leaders via their Annual Global CEO Survey and found that leaders expect more insights than they actually receive.

Figure 5.1 CEOs expect more information than they receive from HR

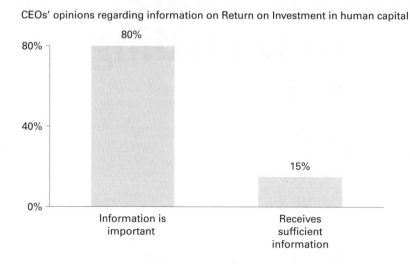

CEOs' opinions regarding information on Return on Investment in human capital

As shown in Figure 5.1, there is a huge disparity between what they deem as important information regarding the ROI of human capital and the amount of information that they actually receive.[2]

Lack of confidence persists in the C-suite and even among line leaders. In Figure 5.2 it is clear that only 12 per cent of CFOs are confident or highly confident that HR and learning and development are spending the right amounts in the right places.[3] Figure 5.3 shows that among line leaders, only 23 per cent agree or strongly agree that they are satisfied with the overall effectiveness of the learning and development function.[4] In other words, more than three-quarters of all line leaders are not satisfied with learning and development's ability to prepare employees for their roles.

Figure 5.2 CFOs lack confidence in HR/L&D spend

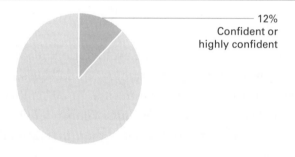

12%
Confident or
highly confident

Figure 5.3 Line leaders are not satisfied with effectiveness of L&D

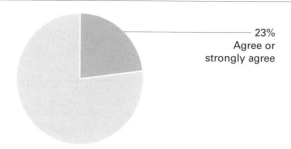

23%
Agree or
strongly agree

Lack of confidence comes from many sources. Without a doubt, one of those sources is the fact that it is hard to measure human activities and motivations with accuracy. Setting that aside, there are the more practical issues that further decrease confidence: organizations do not have systems in place to measure the impact of training, they do not have resources dedicated to measuring impact and they do not have standard models for reporting results.[5]

When it comes to the issue of reporting, often business leaders do not understand the measures that are important to L&D leaders (eg Kirkpatrick's Four Levels of Evaluation), and similarly, L&D leaders struggle with communicating L&D's effectiveness in business terms. The Center for Talent Reporting (www.centerfortalentreporting.org) is working to alleviate this problem, advocating the use of Talent Development Reporting Principles as a framework for reporting. Chapter 8 examines this topic in greater detail. Suffice it to say, L&D is not communicating with business leaders as well as other business units are.

As mentioned in Chapter 2, there is a disconnect between the information that L&D is able to provide to the C-suite and what the C-Suite wants. The top five types of data that L&D provides include the following:[6]

- training expense per employee;
- satisfaction with training;
- training hours per FTE;
- external vendor expense;
- L&D cost per FTE.

According to the ROI Institute, the information that business leaders want focuses on the following three areas:[7]

- Application: how can we increase application of new skills on the job?
- Results: to what degree will a learning programme improve a specific business outcome?
- Value: what will be the return on the learning investment?

The CEB team recommends monitoring scrap learning as a metric that leaders will find valuable. What is scrap? It is learning that is delivered but not applied back on the job. Scrap is measured by asking learners how much training they will apply when they return to the job. If learners indicate they will apply 40 per cent of what they learned, then scrap equals 100 per cent minus 40 per cent, or 60 per cent. For more than 15 years, MTM has measured scrap as a leading indicator of programme quality. Leaders value this metric because it is the inverse of application and without application learning events cannot influence individual and organizational performance. Scrap is a direct indicator of application and a leading indicator of results and value.

Based on millions of data points, Metrics That Matter™ finds that scrap learning averages 45 per cent across all corporate universities that do not measure the effectiveness of training. This benchmark is determined by examining the scrap rate for new users of the Metrics That Matter™ system. Figure 5.4 shows that scrap is pervasive across industries.[8] With nearly half of all training going to waste, it is no wonder that business leaders are concerned about the quality of L&D efforts.

Metrics That Matter™ tracks another important metric that correlates with scrap: performance improvement. While scrap is measured with a simple question, performance improvement is measured using a series of questions that align to the Phillips' ROI Methodology. The resultant value is an estimate of the actual performance improvement that learners expect as a result of the development programme. This approach was described in Chapter 4, but it is repeated here as a reminder. In order to estimate how much training improves

Figure 5.4 Scrap learning rates across industries

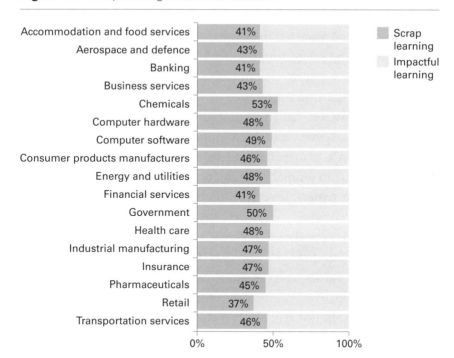

Industry	Scrap learning
Accommodation and food services	41%
Aerospace and defence	43%
Banking	41%
Business services	43%
Chemicals	53%
Computer hardware	48%
Computer software	49%
Consumer products manufacturers	46%
Energy and utilities	48%
Financial services	41%
Government	50%
Health care	48%
Industrial manufacturing	47%
Insurance	47%
Pharmaceuticals	45%
Retail	37%
Transportation services	46%

Legend: Scrap learning / Impactful learning

performance, the post-training survey should ask learners to estimate three things:

1 How much do they expect their performance will improve related to the content of the course due to all factors including the development programme?

2 How much of that improvement is due to the development programme only?

3 How much work time is actually spent on tasks related to the development programme?

Learners respond to these questions using a scale that ranges from 0 per cent to 100 per cent at 10 per cent increments; responses are gathered from learners on post-event surveys immediately after training. Responses are also gathered on a follow-up survey 60 days after training, but for this analysis Metrics That Matter™ relies on the post-event results to maximize the number of responses to both the scrap question and performance improvement questions. The percentage values from each question are multiplied together. This value is then adjusted downward by 35 per cent to account for response bias and overestimation. In this way, the learners estimate their performance improvement, isolate the influence of training and isolate how much training relates to the job. The process is called 'estimation, isolation, isolation and adjustment' or EIIA. Reflecting back to Chapter 4, these estimated (not actual) values provide reasonable rigour while also providing information about application, results and value in a timely manner.

As one might expect, if scrap is high, then performance improvement is low. Likewise, if scrap is low, performance improvement is high – relatively speaking. (It is rare to see a performance improvement value higher than 30 per cent because the EIIA calculation produces small values.) Figure 5.5 shows a scatter plot of scrap and performance improvement for over 300 clients and 18 million evaluation ratings. Each dot represents a client. As expected, a high scrap rate of 45 per cent (eg left side of the X-axis, which has been reversed

Figure 5.5 Scatterplot of scrap vs performance improvement

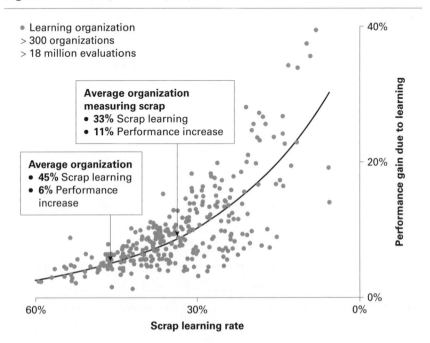

– high scrap is left and low scrap is right) produces a low performance improvement rate of 6 per cent. These values are for organizations when they begin using Metrics That Matter™. After using Metrics That Matter™, scrap falls to 33 per cent and performance improvement rises to 11 per cent for the average organization. As scrap decreases, performance increases. Organizations reduce scrap through monitoring and management of the curriculum.

Is there magic behind the measurement? Does the process of measuring learning cause reductions in scrap and increases in performance? The answer to both questions is no. But measurement often leads to better monitoring and management. Organizations that begin measuring the impact of training often create continuous improvement processes. Remember, the two main reasons to measure training are: 1) determine the effectiveness of training, and 2) continuously improve the quality of courses. Scrap is measured as a key metric in the continuous improvement process. When scrap is measured systematically across the curriculum, it can be monitored using scorecards and/or dashboards. Once it is monitored, it can be managed. Metrics That Matter™ advocates that clients do the following to track scrap and improve performance:

- Measure all courses in the curriculum using the same tools and questions; this ensures that data is comparable and results can be aggregated and compared.

- Create a spread sheet or dashboard that displays a small number of critical metrics (eg scrap, performance improvement and worthwhile investment) for each course.

- Create a useful set of business rules that will guide continuous improvement processes. An example would be:

  - For the top 5 per cent of courses, reinvest in them; do not strive to improve them; continue deploying them as they are; if any changes are made, make changes that will reduce costs without reducing benefits, thereby increasing the ROI for the courses.

  - For the bottom 10 per cent, retire any courses that are no longer aligned to business needs; for those that are aligned but have stale content or need improvement, reinvest to revise them.

– For the remaining 85 per cent of the courses in the middle, continue deploying them but invest in targeted revisions that are designed to reduce scrap and maximize impact.

The business rules may vary from organization to organization or curriculum to curriculum, but the continuous improvement process needs such rules to be effective. Using a process like this produces results and in this way, the curriculum will improve over time. Overall scrap for the curriculum will decrease and performance will increase.

Scrap and performance improvement have a substantial monetary effect on an organization. Scrap is an indicator of wasted learning – money is lost because training is not used. Reducing scrap saves money. On the flip side of the same coin, performance improvement means greater productivity which means the organization adds to its bottom line. Figure 5.6 displays a table that quantifies the value an organization realizes when scrap is reduced (cost savings) and performance is improved (productivity increases).

The example in Figure 5.6 represents an organization with 10,000 employees that is just beginning to measure the effectiveness of its curriculum. The scrap rate is 45 per cent and the performance improvement rate is 6 per cent. The costs of scrap are computed by multiplying the average cost of training per learner as defined by ATD's *State of the Industry Report*[9] ($1195) by the number of employees (10,000) and by 45 per cent. The organization is wasting $5.4 million due to scrap! Despite scrap, training is improving performance by 6 per cent. A rough value for improving performance is based on the change in productivity per dollar invested in the employee. In other words, when performance is improved by 6 per cent, a financial impact can be determined by multiplying the average salary of employees ($60,000) by the number of employees (10,000) and by 6 per cent. Training adds $36 million dollars in productivity! This is substantial and highly valuable – a material amount in auditing terms. But is it worth considering how much money the organization would save if scrap was reduced from 45 per cent to the benchmark of 33 per cent and if performance improvement rose from 6 per cent to the benchmark of 11 per cent. The scrap and performance improvement values are calculated in the second row of the table ($3.9M and $66M respectively.) The difference between two values in the two rows represents the current unrealized value for the organization. If scrap can be reduced to 33 per cent, the organization will save $1.5 million. If performance improves from 6 to 11 per cent, the organization will gain $30 million in productivity. When combined, the organization will realize $31.5 million in value.

Figure 5.6 Monetary impact of reducing scrap and increasing performance improvement

	Waste in learning budget due to scrap	Value of performance improvement due to learning
Average organization	$5.4 million 45% scrap × $1,195 spend per learning × 10,000 employees	$36 million 6% performance improvement × $60,000 average salary × 10,000 employees
Average organization measuring scrap	$3.9 million 33% scrap × $1,195 spend per learner × 10,000 employees	$66 million 11% performance improvement × $60,000 average salary × 10,000 employees
Unrealized gains for average organization	**$1.5 million** in waste	**$30 million** in opportunity costs

Running L&D like a business

One of the ancillary benefits of collecting effectiveness data in MTM is that it provides information that can help L&D run the development function like a business – similar to all of the other operational groups in the organization. The operations group monitors the capital it is given to execute the processes for creating products. It monitors the amount and quality of the product produced and eventually ties the capital inputs and product outputs to business impact. Once the L&D function begins measuring and monitoring inputs, quality, and influence on business measures, L&D leaders can begin running the function like a business. Dave Vance provides excellent guidance on using data to help transform the L&D function from a cost centre to a business partner in his book, *The Business of Learning*.[10]

Reporting on scrap learning

As mentioned in Chapter 3, systems are doing more heavy lifting now than ever before. They are gathering data, storing it and analysing it faster than analysts can process it manually. Efficiency is one of the greatest benefits of implementing an analytics system. When standard data sets are collected, standard analytic routines can be established so reports are produced weekly, daily or even hourly. The analytics that once took days by hand are now done in seconds by various systems.

The primary benefit of in-system processing is that it saves time and effort by performing the administrative tasks of analysis and reporting. In the learning industry, nearly 80 per cent of an analyst's time is spent creating evaluation forms, distributing them, compiling and analysing data and finally creating reports. The remaining 20 per cent is spent interpreting the results, making recommendations and taking action.

A system that automates most of the administrative tasks in the evaluation process up-ends that ratio. Twenty per cent of the analyst's time is spent on administrative tasks and 80 per cent is dedicated to interpreting the results to draw conclusions and to provide insights to stakeholders. The value of analytics comes from interpretation and action. In-system analytic processing transforms the analyst's role so that interpretation and action, not analysis, are the value-generating tasks.

Businesses are starting to realize the value of insights produced by analytics systems that produce business intelligence associated with predictive analytics. Speed to action is also a benefit when systems put information in the hands of end users. Business examples abound, but here are two that might be familiar. If you enrol in Mint.com, the financial system analyses your spending patterns and makes recommendations for saving money by suggesting revisions to your spending habits. Netflix takes the inputs from your movie ratings and recommends other movies you might like. The ratings of other viewers with preferences similar to yours are also included in the analysis. Data becomes information. Information becomes recommendations. Recommendations become actions.

For over a decade, Metrics That Matter™ (MTM) has been auto-mating the survey distribution and reporting process, so learning and talent management professionals can spend more time taking data-driven action than administering the evaluation process. MTM allows users to set up a routine to run a report on a set date and dynamically distribute that report by e-mail to a wide variety of stakeholders who may want to view the same data. Additionally, the Dashboard Module within the system automatically updates the graphic reports on the users' custom dashboards at set intervals and provides the user with filtering capabilities to drill into the organization's data.

MTM puts business intelligence in the hands of end users with a dashboard called Instant Insights™ which focuses on scrap learning. Instant Insights™ follows a simple three-step process that provides immediate value. Figure 5.7 represents the process graphically.

Figure 5.7 Three-step value chain for Instant Insights™

How can scrap be reduced?

As mentioned earlier, the value of measuring scrap is that it pro-vides a metric that can be monitored. More importantly, L&D leaders who monitor the measure can manage it. They can take action to continuously improve the quality of training and reduce scrap. In Chapter 3, we discussed why technology systems are valu-able. Often they make processes more efficient, but the truly valuable business intelligence systems turn data into actionable information. Moreover, they provide recommendations for action. Metrics That Matter™ does exactly this – it analyses the evaluation data collected for clients, provides scrap rates and identifies the drivers of scrap and prescribes actions that L&D can take to make improvements.

Figure 5.8 shows a simple dashboard within Metrics That Matter™ which displays the scrap rate for a programme. Although the figure

Figure 5.8 Instant Insights™ dashboard

Scrap Learning 📊 🗙

43%

Benchmark: 27%

A

Scrap Learning
What insights can you leverage to find potential cost savings?

.all Support Tools ⊘ B

Question: The participant materials (manual, presentation handouts, job aids, etc.) will be useful on the job.

Investment

Recommendations C

The majority of learning takes place outside of the classroom or elearning environment. Ensure that your learning programs provide useful post-training support tools, such as job aids, performance support tools, communities of practice, and knowledge bases. Emphasize the design and development of these resources at least as much in your program development process as the program itself.

Medium

Incorporate in your design and development learner needs that go beyond simply learning to do something for the first time. Provide resources that address additional needs such as when they go to apply what they have learned, but may have forgotten some details, as well as when they need more depth to address a more complex or challenging scenario.

Medium

.all Alignment
This training aligns with the business priorities and goals identified by my organization.

.all Support Tools
I will be provided adequate resources (time, money, equipment) to successfully apply this training on my job.

.all Courseware
The scope of the material was appropriate to my needs.

A

 ⊘ Help

43%

Benchmark: 27%

Data as of: Mar 12, 2014
Next data refresh: Apr 3, 2014

D

Potential Savings ⊘

$4,433,437

of estimated potential savings over the next year.

here is printed in black and white, the online version uses red and green colour coding to signal areas of strength and opportunity. The red box (labelled A) displays a scrap rate that is 43 per cent for the organization. The box is red because scrap is higher than the benchmark of 27 per cent (shown in fine print in the box). If the scrap rate were lower (better) than benchmark, the box would be green. Directly below the red box, 'Support Tools' (labelled B) appears in large bold letters. The MTM system has analysed all of the post-event evaluation results within the organization's account and determined that Support Tools is the factor that drives scrap. This factor is determined by the responses to the statement, 'The participant materials (manuals, presentation handouts, job aids, etc) will be useful on the job.' So, when attendees do not have support tools (eg course materials), scrap goes up and when they do have support (eg provide high ratings), scrap goes down.

How can this information be used to reduce scrap? In the section directly below Support Tools, there is a set of recommendations (labelled C). These are best practices that can be applied to revise programmes with the intent of improving support tools. These recommendations change based on the driver that is listed above. So if 'Worthwhile Investment' were determined to be the driver, the list of recommendations would change to reflect actions that designers could take to improve worthwhile investment. The recommendations are system-generated.

Additional drivers of scrap are listed below the recommendations. In this case, the drivers relate to alignment, support tools and courseware. It is not surprising that poor alignment, support and courseware leads to suboptimal learning. If instructional designers improve these factors, ratings will improve and so will scrap.

The last piece of useful information provided on the Instant Insights™ dashboard is the potential savings (labelled D). This is the amount that the organization will realize in savings and productivity if the current scrap rate is reduced to the benchmark value.

The dashboard can be customized to show the entire curriculum or a subset of classes like leadership, sales, instructor-led training, virtual training or other aspects as long as demographic data is collected for those courses.

Is the Instant Insights™ dashboard sufficient for continuous improvement? Certainly not, but it is a great monitoring tool to allow L&D leaders to view what is happening at a macro level in real time. In order to maximize the continuous improvement process, L&D managers should examine the programmes that are under-performing by running additional reports within Metrics That Matter™. Of course, this continuous improvement process can be implemented with any system that is collecting evaluation data. Metrics That Matter™ simply makes it easier given its dashboard and reporting capabilities.

The drivers of scrap vary per organization. Some can be controlled by L&D and others cannot. Figure 5.9 displays many of the things that can influence scrap. Those on the left side are more directly shaped by the L&D organization, such as ineffective delivery and content quality. Those on the right are less influenced by L&D and more by the broader organization, such as low learner motivation and no opportunity to apply. In the following sections, we'll discuss some of the most common drivers of scrap and how organizations can address them.

Scrap and manager engagement

Data from Metrics That Matter™ show that manager support is one of the lowest-scoring areas on a SmartSheet, meaning most organizations do not have good manager support before and after learning events. When Metrics That Matter™ began measuring manager support, it was intended to help L&D professionals prove that in some cases the context and design of the programme were effective, and to help them pinpoint where the real problem was. Often business owners would scratch their heads when they deployed development programmes and performance did not improve. By measuring programme effectiveness and manager support, L&D leaders can show that their efforts are working but managers are not providing appropriate support. In this way, L&D can easily say, 'Training is not the problem.'

Figure 5.9 Factors that influence scrap learning

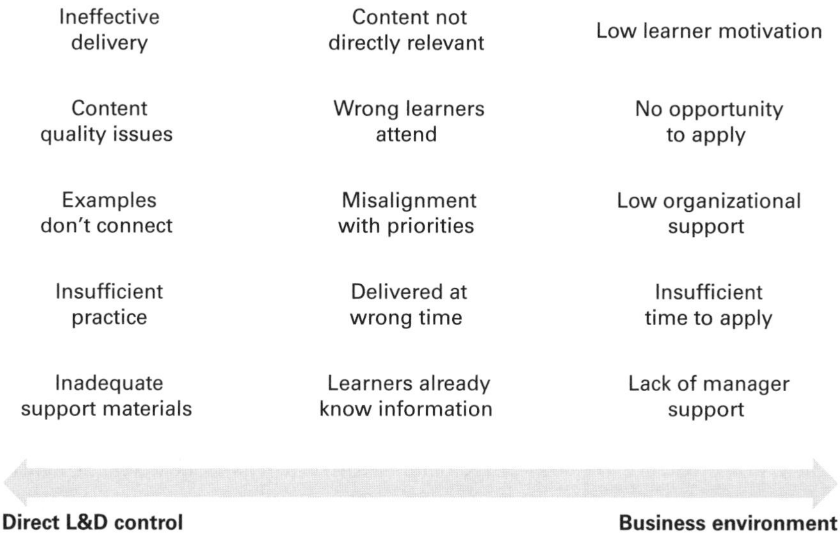

Ineffective delivery	Content not directly relevant	Low learner motivation
Content quality issues	Wrong learners attend	No opportunity to apply
Examples don't connect	Misalignment with priorities	Low organizational support
Insufficient practice	Delivered at wrong time	Insufficient time to apply
Inadequate support materials	Learners already know information	Lack of manager support

Direct L&D control   **Business environment**

Archimedes wrote, 'Give me a lever long enough and a fulcrum on which to place it, and I can move the world.' Manager support is one of the factors that can increase the length of the lever – or prevent its length from decreasing as learning is lost. Figure 5.10 represents manager support as a factor that extends the training lever that improves performance.

Research shows that there is a relationship between manager support before and after training and improved performance. One study investigated a variety of roles that managers play in the learning and performance process. Five were measured and linked to performance:[11]

- evaluating learner readiness before attending training;
- setting expectations for learning before training begins;
- getting involved with application of training after the learner attends;
- following up on expectations that were set before training;
- providing necessary resources to support performance.

The study collected data via an industry-wide survey and the results were surprising – but not in the positive way that one might expect, as shown in Figures 5.11–5.16.

Figure 5.10 Manager support extends training as a performance improvement lever

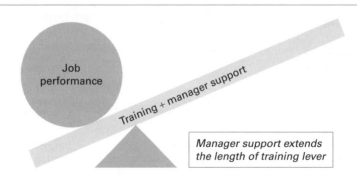

Job performance

Training + manager support

> Manager support extends
> the length of training lever

Manager involvement begins with examining learner readiness. For some courses like onboarding, no examination is necessary. All new employees need some level of onboarding to learn culture, proprietary processes and tools. As employees gain tenure and as they differentiate in their roles, some programmes are more relevant to job responsibilities than others. Some programmes are necessary while others are optional. Whether required or optional, it is the manager's responsibility to determine if a learning event will be valuable for the individual and for the organization. The manager should answer questions like, 'Is this person ready for this new set of skills?' 'Will the person be successful with these new skills?' and 'Does the organization need this person to acquire new knowledge and skills to become more productive?' When the answer to these questions is 'Yes', the person is ready. If the answer is 'No', the person is not ready. If the person is not ready and the manager approves attendance, there is a high likelihood that the knowledge and skills gained will not be applied. Learning will turn to scrap and will not be valuable to the organization.

Sending the right person to a development programme is essential, but Figure 5.11 shows that only 21 per cent of organizations preassess learners 'most of the time' or 'all of the time' prior to sending them. Said differently, 79 per cent of organizations do *not* have a culture of pre-assessment for learner readiness, thus increasing the chances that learning will not be well-targeted and will result in scrap. It is no wonder that scrap is 45 per cent for many organizations.

Figure 5.11 How often do managers assess readiness for development programmes?

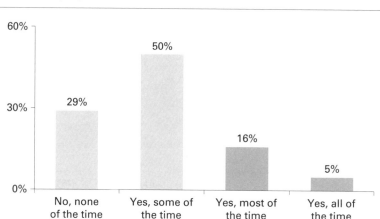

Another important role that managers play is to set expectations with the learner prior to the event. This consists of a simple conversation, but it requires that the manager understand the objectives of the course and how it will improve job performance. Like a parent who sets behavioural expectations with children, managers are responsible for explaining that training is not a liberal arts education. Training is not designed as a broad-based, philosophically driven approach to development. It is designed to deliver information about specific knowledge and to improve specific skills related to a particular job role. When expectations are set in this way, learners are more likely to attend to course content and make connections between classroom situations and on-the-job requirements.

Figure 5.12 shows that managers rarely set expectations among learners before they attend development programmes. For 75 per cent of organizations, expectations are set 25 per cent of the time or less. Only 9 per cent of organizations set expectations most of the time (75 to 100 per cent of the time).

After learners attend development programmes, managers have several opportunities to be influential. Simply getting involved after the programme is a start. Involvement takes many forms, and three specific behaviours are shown in Figure 5.13. Those behaviours are on a gradient from low involvement – 'I have little involvement' – to high involvement – 'I will hold my employees accountable.' Unfortunately, a large portion (44 per cent) of organizations have low manager

Figure 5.12 How often are expectations set before development programmes?

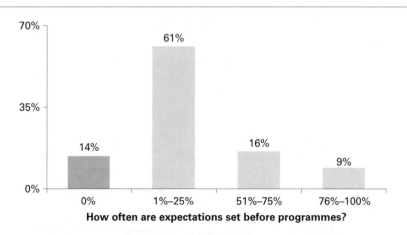

How often are expectations set before programmes?

Figure 5.13 How do managers get involved after development programmes?

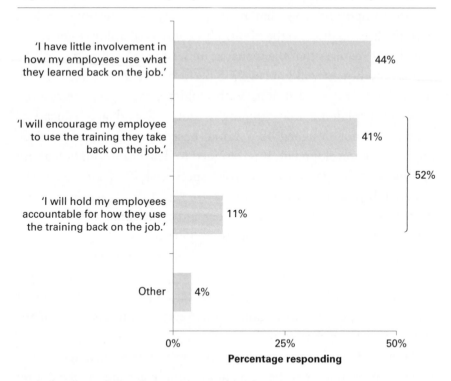

involvement after training. A similar proportion (41 per cent) are slightly more involved, encouraging employees to apply training back on the job. In contrast, a very small percentage (11 per cent) actually hold employees accountable for applying training back on the job. In other words, slightly more than half (52 per cent) of managers make a small to moderate effort to reduce scrap and increase productivity on the job. Such discouraging results beg the questions, 'How much effort is really required to provide encouragement?' and 'How much effort is required to monitor performance and ensure that training is used on the job?' We don't have answers to these questions here, but it seems that slightly more effort could have a substantial impact.

In Figure 5.12 it is clear that expectations setting before programmes is low. Likewise, after programmes, managers do very little to follow up on expectations. Figure 5.14 shows five specific ways that managers follow up. At the simplest level, managers require a summary debrief of the event. At the most complex level, managers require learners to apply knowledge and skills and demonstrate a measurable impact on a business result. As the complexity of the required action increases, the percentage of managers who require the action decreases. The most complex requirement, 'measurement of a business result change', was least often selected, at 13 per cent. Said differently, only 13 per cent of managers require learners to demonstrate with evidence that training had an actual benefit for the business.

Figure 5.14 How do managers follow up on expectations after programmes?

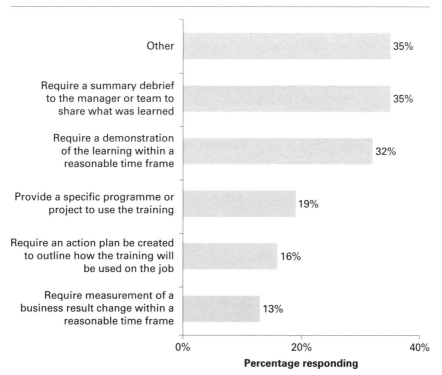

Managers are also responsible for providing resources that employees need in order to be successful on the job. Just as parents buy books and school supplies for their children, managers must provide tools for employees. If an employee attends an Excel programme and returns to her job but does not have Excel on her computer, she cannot be expected to apply what she learned and improve her performance. Similarly, managers are responsible for creating the opportunities for employees to apply skills in new situations. An employee who gains new management skills needs to have the opportunity to manage. Importantly, not every attempt to apply learning is successful, and a failed attempt is often discouraging. Managers should monitor performance, provide guidance and encourage continued attempts especially after initial failures. In this way, managing learner performance is akin to professional parenting.

Figure 5.15 shows the various ways that managers provide performance support. Shockingly, each of the actions in the table is only performed by 25 per cent of respondents or fewer.

Figure 5.15 How do managers provide resources to support performance?

Figure 5.16 Summary of manager support before and after programmes

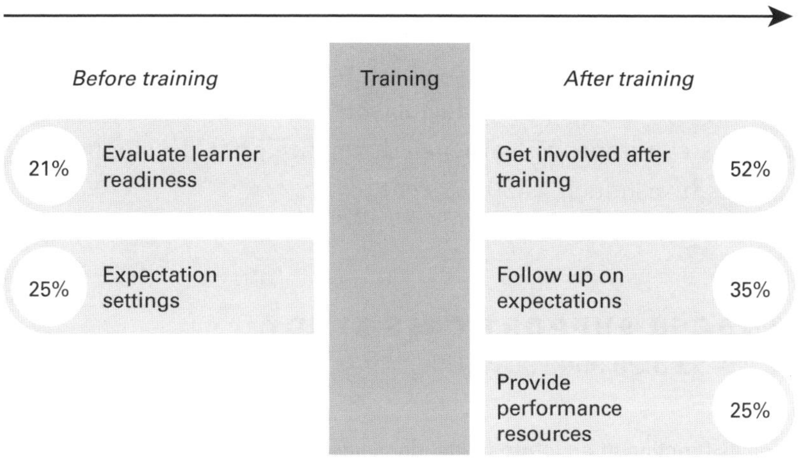

Figure 5.16 provides a quick summary of the research results shared so far. For some organizations, the level of manager support across the five areas might be high and encouraging. For others, it might be astoundingly low. No matter how you cut it, the *average* results are discouragingly low. It appears that there is absentee parenting in most organizations. There is still substantial room for improvement across all five aspects of support. Improvement will ensure that the right people attend development programmes and that expectations are set before learning begins. Manager support afterwards will help employees apply what they learn and encourage them to hone and refine skills even when they are not initially successful. Manager involvement will reduce scrap and improve performance, providing efficiency and productivity gains without even stepping into the classroom.

A recent film documentary, *When the Game Stands Tall*, chronicled the achievements of the De La Salle High School football team in California, which won 151 consecutive games. In the first few minutes of the film, there is a powerful scene where a senior stands in the locker room with his teammates and coaches and reads from an index card. That card contains some lofty goals – all of which he achieved during the season. In that moment we see a simple yet powerful performance tool – public goal setting, public performance and public account-ability to self, coaches and the team. His presentation is also followed by public encouragement and praise for achieving his goals.

How would organizational performance be different if managers took a more active role in coaching (parenting) direct reports? Research shows that learners who feel they have manager support improve their performance by 17.5 per cent. Research from CEB Learning and Development Leadership Council finds that effective managers can improve learner performance after development programmes by as much as 20 per cent.

MANAGER SUPPORT CASE STUDY
Prep Up, Step Up and Follow Up

The sales function at an international consumer packaged goods company has a unique internal support group dedicated to serving the performance development needs of its sales professionals who in turn drive the business outcomes for the organization. Their learning strategy is designed to deliver ongoing, increased performance through a three-step framework called 'Prep Up, Step Up, Follow Up', which exemplifies a systematic approach to incorporating manager support into the learning process.

Prep Up. In this phase, the employee ensures readiness to achieve learning objectives and aligns with the manager for coaching, affirmation and confirmation that the learning objectives are on target and will enable the employee to deliver improved performance and the required business results. Two to three weeks prior to participating in a strategic programme, learners are required to meet with their manager to review the syllabus and complete a pre-learning impact plan. It is an agreement between the learner and the manager on what they are going to learn and how it can be applied on the job. It also represents the contract for learning between the employee and the manager to ensure the employee is ready to attend. The manager confirms that the learning objectives are on target and will enable the employee to deliver improved performance and required business results. This phase is owned by the learner and supported by the manager. Nearly 100 per cent of all sales professionals complete their pre-learning impact plans.

Step Up. During this phase, the learner attends the programme and monitors whether it provides the necessary knowledge and skills to improve on-the-job performance. Learners are charged with identifying a business opportunity or personal development area to which they will apply their learning. This allows them to work through their individual needs while applying the content they are learning to ensure it becomes a working session. With application already started against their business gap, they feel confident in continuing the application of learning on the job. This phase is jointly owned by the employee and the learning tool (e-learning, instructor-led training, colleges, etc), but the learner is always the ultimate owner of the learning objectives. The employee has to come to the training prepared to learn, ready to apply current knowledge, ready to integrate new knowledge and determined to apply new learning to business priorities.

Follow Up. After the learner completes the programme, the manager checks in within 45 days to determine if performance support systems are being used, to provide feedback on performance and to coach professionals towards higher levels of performance. This phase is owned by all. As a contract, it ties the employee, the manager, the L&D team and the organization together. This truly is the only way to deliver the business strategy. Once the employee has used one of the learning tools, she is instructed to confirm her learning objectives with a manager, share knowledge gained and share how the knowledge will enable her to deliver on the business strategy.

The strategic framework of Prep Up, Step Up and Follow Up is designed to deliver an ongoing cycle of skill development, improved performance and delivery on business results. It engages and drives support of the employee by the manager to utilize learning and focus on learning for growth, development and delivering business results that lead to competitive advantage for the organization.

Conclusion

Learning organizations sometimes find it difficult to determine the right measure to instantly convey curriculum quality. Scrap learning is a valuable metric to fit that need. It provides insight about the amount of learning that is being applied (or not being applied) on the job. It is also strongly related to performance improvement; as scrap decreases, performance increases. As a leading indicator of quality, it is influenced by other factors like instructor quality, courseware quality, relevance of materials, etc. By taking apart what is causing scrap within a curriculum, L&D groups can implement a continuous improvement process that will save money (eg reduce scrap) as well as generate revenue by increasing productivity (eg improve performance). Reducing scrap and improving performance are not limited to influencers inside the classroom. This chapter has examined five ways that managers can influence scrap and performance without setting foot inside the classroom.

Endnotes

1 Robert K Branson, Gail T Rayner, J Lamarr Cox, John P Furman, F J King and Wallace H Hannum (1975) *Interservice Procedures for Instructional Systems Development* (5 vols) TRADOC (Pam 350–30) US Army Training and Doctrine Command, Fort Monroe, VA.

2 PwC (2012) 15th Annual Global CEO Survey 2012, Delivering results: growth and value in a volatile world, PwC [online] https://www.pwc.com/gx/en/ceo-survey/pdf/15th-global-pwc-ceo-survey.pdf.

3 CEB (2014) Finance Leadership Council, Overhead cost management survey.

4 CEB (2011) Learning and Development Leadership Council, L&D team capabilities survey.

5 John R Mattox II (2013) Drivers of talent analytics, whitepaper, KnowledgeAdvisors, October, Chicago, IL.

6 CEB (2013) Corporate Leadership Council, The analytics era: transforming HR's impact on the business.

7 Jack Phillips and Patti Phillips (2010) How executives view learning metrics, *Chief Learning Officer*, December.

8 CEB Training Effectiveness Dashboard (2014) N = 27,095.

9 Association for Talent Development (2013) *2013 State of the Industry Report*, ATD.

10 David L Vance (2010) *The Business of Learning: How to manage corporate training to improve your bottom line*, Poudre River Press, Windsor, CO.

11 John R Mattox II (2010) Manager engagement: reducing scrap learning, *Training Industry Quarterly*, Fall, pp 29–33 [online] http://www.cedma-europe.org/newsletter%20articles/TrainingOutsourcing/Manager%20Engagement%20-%20Reducing%20Scrap%20Learning%20(Oct%202010).pdf.

Access to the CEB resources cited in this book is limited to members. For information about membership, please contact CEB's Member Support Centre at CEB.Support@cebglobal.com or +1-866-913-2632.

Aligning L&D to business goals through needs assessment   06

Measure twice, cut once

Ensure a link between training content and business needs

In Chapter 5 we discussed research indicating that CEOs, CFOs and frontline leaders have information needs about the effectiveness of training. Unfortunately, these leaders are often disappointed with the information that is available and with the ability of L&D solutions to provide knowledge and skills that will improve performance on the job. There are many ways to solve this problem. The foremost is to align training to business needs. In its simplest form, alignment involves measuring a business unit's strengths and performance gaps at an individual level by gathering and analysing data and then filling those gaps with highly targeted learning solutions.

At this point it is worthwhile diving deeper into one aspect of analytics that contributes substantially to the quality of development programmes and performance improvement. That aspect is learning needs assessment. It is designed to determine if the knowledge and skill gaps that can be closed by development programmes are critical to achieving the organization's business goals. As we proceed, let's assume that a performance consultant has spoken with stakeholders and determined that training is in fact the solution that is needed. When conducted well, needs assessment is designed to identify knowledge, skill and ability gaps among employees, both as individuals and groups. Once identified, development programmes can be designed to close those gaps. Assuming training is implemented as planned and knowledge and skills are transferred, employees should perform better after the learning event than before. In turn, the individual and the organization should become more productive. Needs assessment is designed to identify the knowledge and skills that go furthest to drive business outcomes.

How is alignment achieved?

Aligning the learning and development needs within an organization is no small feat, yet it is critical for L&D to undertake if it intends to demonstrate value to the organization. The ADDIE process, which is discussed in more detail later, is one of several approaches that can be used to align one or a small number of courses to a specific set of knowledge and skill gaps. Given the growing complexity of most organizations, a similar process would be helpful for aligning the entire L&D function's portfolio to the business strategy.

In an article published in 2014 in *T+D Magazine*, Diane Valenti recommends four questions to align development programmes with strategic objectives.[1] Those questions are:

- What is the organization's goal for the coming fiscal year?
- What tactics do you plan to employ to achieve this goal?
- Who will be implementing these tactics?
- What new knowledge and/or skills do you anticipate they will need to implement these tactics?

These questions provide a useful structure, but this approach may be too simple for some complex organizations. An alternative approach is Jay Bahlis' whitepaper, Maximize Training Impact by Aligning to Business Goals.[2] In it he explains multiple ways to gain alignment with organizational goals (see Figure 6.1). Bahlis starts at the organizational level (left side) by understanding its mission and goals. This understanding cascades to the division or business unit level as well.

Figure 6.1 Process for aligning development programmes with organizational goals

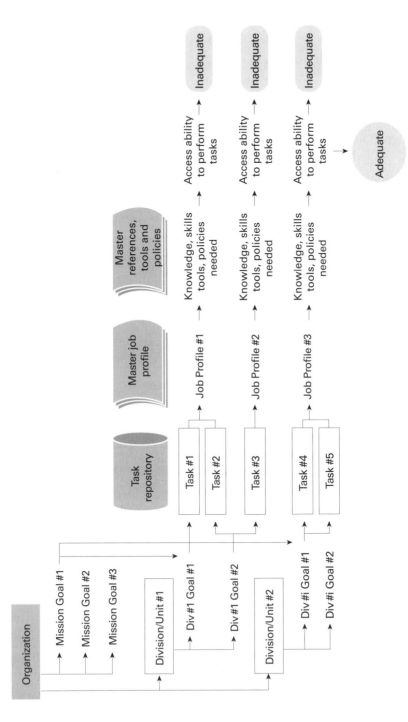

SOURCE: adapted from Bahlis (2014)

Moving to the right, the next step is to determine the tasks that align to the specific goals for each division goal. Then the tasks are aligned to a job profile. Next, the job profiles are examined for the knowledge, skills, tools and policies that are applied to perform the tasks. Finally, individuals are assessed to determine if they have the ability to perform the tasks. If their abilities are inadequate, an intervention, such as a development programme, will have to be designed to close the gap. Depending on the organization, Valenti's or Bahlis' approaches could provide the right guidance for gaining alignment. Critical components to both approaches include: determining the organizational needs (possibly the business unit needs); determining the tasks/job profiles that align to the needs; determining the target audience; determining what knowledge and skill gaps need to be addressed; and determining what methods might be best for filling the gaps.

Dave Vance, the Managing Director of the Center for Talent Reporting, describes alignment that is achieved through strategic needs assessment as 'the proactive process of ensuring that learning is carefully planned and directed to meet the highest priority goals of an organization'.[3] He also describes the ideal organizational alignment in the following way:

> At the organizational level, HR is a valued, strategic business partner
> that supports the organization's most important goals by partnering
> with goal owners and business unit leaders to help them achieve their
> goals. This is achieved by having proactive meetings with the CEO
> and other senior leaders, by reaching agreement on planned initiatives
> and their expected impact on the business, and by holding each other
> accountable to measuring for outcomes.[4]

At the departmental level, the HR department leader manages his or her function with the same degree of business discipline that peers apply in other departments. This entails creating a plan for the year with SMART goals for the department to achieve the desired improvement, using reports containing key HR measures to review progress against a plan every month, and taking appropriate action to get back on plan when needed.

Vance recommends asking the following questions, which are somewhat similar to Valenti's, in order to facilitate the process for aligning goals and aligning L&D to meet them:

- Do you know your organization's top five goals?
  - Do you know which are the most important to the CEO?
- Do you meet with senior leaders each year to discuss if/how HR (L&D) can support them?
- Do you have SMART goals for your department?
  - Have you identified the 5–10 measures and set a plan or target for each one?
- Do your departmental senior leaders meet each month to review progress against the plan?

The ADDIE model: linear vs cyclical business alignment

While there are several instructional design models that can serve to develop training programmes, the most commonly used in US corporate universities is the ADDIE model.[5] The approach, which was developed as a joint effort between Florida State University and the US Air Force, outlines five steps:[6,7]

1 Analyse

In this phase, the business needs are identified and the instructional design team determines if training is in fact the right solution for the situation. Assuming that it is, the analyse phase continues by gathering data to answer a variety of questions about the budget, the target audience, the core knowledge, skills and abilities that need to be transferred, the timelines, acceptable delivery methods and any constraints that exist. Data can be collected through surveys, interviews, focus groups, operational data – any source that can provide insight. This is the most important phase for determining alignment.

2 Design

In this phase, the team creates a working design for the learning solution that will fill knowledge and skill gaps aligned to the business needs. The design encompasses timing, the methodology or methodologies, the courseware, storyboards, exercises, job aids and pre- and post-training support. Learning objectives are documented and modules are structured. Systems such as the learning management system, the e-learning platform and the post-training 'help tools' are incorporated as support for developing, implementing and evaluating the programme.

3 Develop

In this phase, the team transforms the design into action by creating media and courseware, scripting materials and programming systems as needed.

4 Implement

In this phase, the course is deployed to the target audience as specified in the design.

5 Evaluate

In this phase, feedback is gathered from learners, instructors, designers, managers and business stakeholders. The feedback process can be simple, such as a quick conversation with learners and instructors about the quality of the course. Or, as described in Chapter 3, the evaluation could be supported by web-based surveys and could employ an experimental design and operational data to demonstrate performance improvement.

The original ADDIE model published in 1975 was linear, running left to right, with several sub-processes. See Figure 6.2, which is adapted from the original model.[8] For the purposes of this chapter, we want to focus mainly on the Analyse step. This is where the majority of alignment with business needs occurs. As we continue our discussion of alignment, first we will consider the transformation of the linear ADDIE model into the cyclical model. Second, we will touch briefly on ROI estimation during the remaining steps. Both processes are critical for creating alignment as well as creating a clear way to measure alignment as training is delivered.

Figure 6.2 Original ADDIE Model

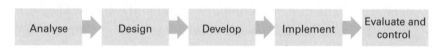

From linear to cyclical in search of ROI

The ADDIE model has evolved over four decades. One change is that the modern ADDIE model has a slightly different label for the last phase compared to the original version. Figure 6.2 shows the last phase was originally labelled Evaluate and Control; the modern version has dropped Control. This is an important distinction because Control means that the evaluation data are acted upon and used to further improve the course and the performance of learners. Control implies that the model is cyclical. Dick and Carry expanded on this notion and explained that a more useful instructional design approach is to consider the design process as a complex system of interacting parts.[9] The systems approach emphasizes that the process should not be linear and that each process step can and should influence the others. More recently the Dick and Carey systems model has been simplified to emphasize alignment of training to business needs as a cyclical process, where all stages interact and influence other stages and where the cycle of alignment repeats over time in order to optimize results. Figure 6.3 is a graphic representation of a cyclical ADDIE process.

Figure 6.3 Representation of ADDIE as a cyclical process

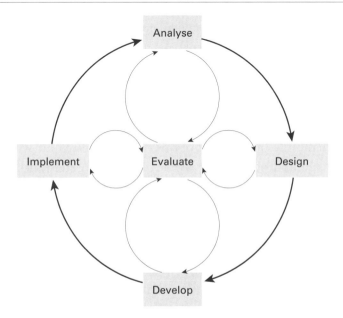

Unpacking the 'Analyse' stage of business alignment

The first step in the ADDIE model is Analyse, and many instructional designers undertake this phase with a needs assessment. Renowned instructional designer Allison Rossett defines training needs assessment in this way:

> Needs assessment is the systematic effort that we make to gather opinions and ideas from a variety of sources on performance problems.[10]

The US Office of Personnel Management (OPM) provides a more comprehensive definition on its website:

> The purpose of a training needs assessment is to identify performance requirements and the knowledge, skills, and abilities needed by an agency's workforce to achieve the requirements. An effective training needs assessment will help direct resources to areas of greatest demand. The assessment should address resources needed to fulfill organizational mission, improve productivity, and provide quality products and services. A needs assessment is the process of identifying the 'gap' between performance required and current performance. When a difference exists, it explores the causes and reasons for the gap and methods for closing or eliminating the gap. A complete needs assessment also considers the consequences of ignoring the gaps.[11]

On the same website, OPM also makes clear the three levels at which business alignment and needs assessment should be considered:

- Organizational assessment evaluates the level of organizational performance. An assessment of this type will determine what skills, knowledge and abilities an agency needs. It determines what is required to alleviate the problems and weaknesses of the agency as well as to enhance strengths and competencies, especially for Mission Critical Occupations (MCO). Organizational assessment takes into consideration various additional factors, including changing demographics, political trends, technology and the economy.[12]

- Occupational assessment examines the skills, knowledge and abilities required for affected occupational groups. Occupational assessment identifies how and which occupational discrepancies or gaps exist, potentially introduced by the new direction of an agency. It also examines new ways to do work that can eliminate the discrepancies or gaps.

- Individual assessment analyses how well an individual employee is doing a job and determines the individual's capacity to do new or different work. Individual assessment provides information on which employees need training and what kind.

At all three levels, needs assessment is a core part of the Analyse phase and, ideally, it requires the instructional design team to collect information about the needs of the business first and those of the individual second. Practically, the design team interviews stakeholders to determine what development needs should be addressed to support the business. Those conversations should also look at how much stakeholders expect that addressing those development needs will improve performance, as it is a critical part of logic modelling and expectation setting.

It is also advisable to collect information about the knowledge and skill gaps of learners from other sources outside the business. Managers can observe performance on the job and report areas where they see major skill gaps. The information can also come from the target population of employees who are potential learners. They can provide feedback about their own skill levels and the perceived value of those skills on the job. Such data can be gathered through surveys, interviews and focus groups, and later in this chapter we will share how a professional services firm used all three to understand skill gaps. We'll also see how a personality assessment can be used to determine gaps and lead to learning paths.

Earlier, we mentioned that the ADDIE model is cyclical. As such, the Evaluation phase often informs the Analyse phase. It may seem odd to include evaluation as a part of the Analyse phase, but it is actually a natural part of the process. Post-training evaluation information provides insights into what has worked and what has not worked in the past. Evaluation results may indicate that the new hires would like more e-learning about their specific business line and their roles prior to attending the standard instructor-led onboarding course. Results might also indicate that the training materials used to date are not appropriate or that a specific instructor is not qualified to deliver the course. Such information is invaluable for improving course quality.

The interaction between each phase in the ADDIE model is also evident during the design phase. When a team considers various design solutions, the options might range from a simple paper-based pamphlet that serves as a job aid to a gamified, multi-player, cloud-based course. The team considers the best possible solution within a given budget. For instance, a game-based solution may be the most effective approach for transferring knowledge and skills because it will have greatest impact on performance, but it may be beyond the budgeted resources and therefore a non-viable solution. Simple cost–benefit discussions within the team are a natural part of the design process when attempting to determine the most cost-effective learning solution. An article from *T+D Magazine*[13] emphasizes that Return on Investment (ROI) is a critical evaluation metric that should be used to make decisions throughout the *entire* ADDIE process.

Traditionally, ROI is used to demonstrate a programme's cost-effectiveness after training has been delivered. ROI should be used to:

- forecast the value of a training programme before it is designed;

- plan the most cost-effective training by selecting the training methods and tools that will maximize learning while minimizing costs;

- demonstrate the effectiveness of training after it has been deployed;

- make decisions about future versions of the programme, especially in comparison to other programmes in the curriculum.

The natural process of considering cost effectiveness while designing a course helps create a product that meets the needs of the business while staying in line with available resources. The process also shows that analysis and evaluation are not reserved for the beginning and the end of the ADDIE model.

How can evaluation results inform the Analyse phase?

Rossi and Freeman describe two types of evaluation: formative and summative.[14] Both are defined below and both are used when determining the value of talent development programmes.

- **Formative evaluation** is a set of monitoring processes. It is used to monitor the implementation of a given programme. If a course targets new hires during their first week of work and consists of a one-day, instructor-led programme, three e-learning modules and four documents, then the formative evaluation would assess whether all new hires attended each aspect of the programme and completed all the requisite components.

- **Summative evaluation** focuses on determining the impact of a given programme. Does the new onboarding programme prepare new hires for their daily tasks that begin during week two? Is the programme more effective than on-the-job training or hiring experienced employees who already know how to perform role-related tasks?

Both types of evaluation are necessary as they help instructional design teams by providing data during the Analyse phase and insights during the Design phase. These evaluation processes indicate whether training was deployed as prescribed and whether there are opportunities to improve courseware and delivery methods.

In order to develop an effective course, instructional designers need to know the drivers of learning. If you polled a group of designers about the things that drive learning, they would likely respond with some or all of the following – relevant materials, good instructors, in-class activities, pertinent examples, time to practise, in-class feedback and high-quality materials, among others. Their opinions would vary on which factors are most important.

Before continuing our discussion about linking evaluation results to the needs assessment process, it is worth examining some of the findings from research about the drivers of effective training. In 2009, Nick Bontis conducted a study to determine which aspects of training programmes lead to learning, application and performance.[15] We shared this research in Chapter 4, but we are revisiting it here with a slightly different perspective – how can evaluation results inform needs analysis?

Bontis examined more than half a million evaluations from the Metrics That Matter™ system from more than 70 companies and developed a structural equation model to determine causal relationships among factors. Results from post-event evaluations (immediately after training) and follow-up evaluations (60 days later) were analysed. Each question on the surveys was aligned to a factor, as shown in Figure 6.4. For example, the statement, 'I learned new knowledge and skills during this programme' aligned to the Learning Effectiveness factor and 'Training was a worthwhile investment for my career development' was one of multiple items that aligned to the Worthwhile Investment factor. Bontis' Predictive Learning Impact Model revealed that the three main drivers of learning are:

- **Instructor Effectiveness** – the quality ratings of instructors based on responses to statements like 'The instructor was effective' and 'The instructor was knowledgeable of the course materials.'

- **Courseware Quality** – the quality ratings of the course materials and the format in which the course was delivered.

- **Worthwhile Investment** – the relevance of the materials as rated by asking whether training was a worthwhile investment.

Among these three factors, Worthwhile Investment is the strongest predictor of learning. That is, if learners believe that training was worth their time to attend, then they were highly likely to indicate that they learned new knowledge and skills. This structural equation model provides more value than other analytic approaches like correlation or regression because it tests multiple relationships among factors simultaneously and determines the optimal causal chain. In this situation, Instructor Effectiveness, Courseware Quality and Worthwhile Investment each contribute directly to Learning Effectiveness. Yet, they are more effective in combination. Learning is optimized when great instructors deliver high-quality course materials that are highly relevant so that learners believe training was a worthwhile investment.

Figure 6.4 Predictive Learning Impact Model

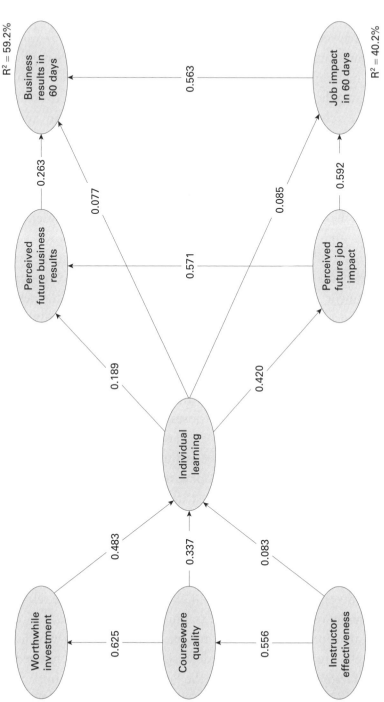

SOURCE: Bontis (2009)

The rest of the model shows that learning leads to expected performance improvement. This is measured immediately after training as Perceived Future Job Impact. Actual Job Impact at 60 days is measured using a follow-up survey in which learners confirm that they have applied skills acquired during training. Lastly, they also indicate whether those skills have led to business improvement.

Research from CEB's Learning and Development Leadership Council supports the message we have shared throughout this chapter: Needs analysis is a critical step for developing programmes that align to business needs, contribute to learning and eventually lead to application and performance improvement.[16] Figure 6.5 shows the three critical areas that bridge the gap between learning events and on-the-job performance. These are: improving needs analysis, building learner motivation and enabling manager support. As with the research conducted by Bontis, relevance (worthwhile investment) is the strongest influencer (29 per cent) in the needs analysis process which leads to business impact. Additionally, manager support also influences on-the-job performance by as much as 20 per cent, which is very similar to the findings we shared in Chapter 5.

With regards to the Analyse phase, both sets of research (Bontis and the L&D Leadership Council) can provide great insight for the design team for planning purposes. The evaluation results *should* inform the Analyse phase whenever the ADDIE model is restarted to revise a course. Notably, the evaluation results do *not* inform the team about stakeholder needs or learner skill gaps, but they do provide insights about how the last iteration of the course did (or did not) fill those needs. If the instructor effectiveness is low, the design team can focus on finding better instructors or training the instructor cadre better. If the courseware ratings are low, the designers can focus on improving the materials. If the ratings are low for worthwhile investment, the team can make the material more relevant and ensure the right people attend training.

Evaluation data also indicates priorities based on which factors have the greatest impact on addressing the development needs. If all three factors on the left side of the Predictive Learning Impact Model (Figure 6.4) need improvement, they should be prioritized in this

Figure 6.5 The key to bridging the learning performance gap

Improve needs analysis

Impact of needs analysis activities on improvement in learner performance

Solution relevance to critical business objectives — 29%
Solution relevance to urgent individual skill gap — 22%
L&D's understanding of daily workflow — 19%
L&D's understanding of the business — 16%
Ownership of solutions and barriers — 18%

Maximum impact

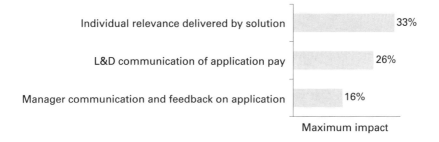

Build learner motivation

Impact of value demonstration activities on learner motivation to apply

Individual relevance delivered by solution — 33%
L&D communication of application pay — 26%
Manager communication and feedback on application — 16%

Maximum impact

Enable manager support

Impact of application support activities on improvement in learner performance

Manager support of employee development — 20%
Opportunities for application created by manager — 10%
Opportunities for application identified by manager — 8%
Change in learned behaviour as assisted by manager — 8%

Maximum impact

order – Worthwhile Investment, Courseware Quality and Instructor Effectiveness – because the factors have the most influence on learning in that order. So the design team should focus on making the course relevant and worthwhile before they attend to improving courseware or instructor quality. Additional information comes from detailed evaluation reports for individual classes which contain qualitative feedback in the form of comments. On many evaluations, learners are asked to respond to questions like 'What was most useful about training?', 'Least useful?' and 'How can training be improved to make it more relevant to your job?' Responses to these questions, especially the last question, provide excellent information to fuel the needs assessment, highlighting areas of opportunity.

What about tests?

Knowledge and skills tests are sometimes part of the summative evaluation process and they provide useful information for the needs assessment. Pre- and post-course tests are used to assess whether learners gained new knowledge and skills during learning events. A well-written test will align to the course objectives and the knowledge and skills gaps defined in the needs assessment. If so, the test can provide insights about the gaps that the course closes and those it does not. As such, this evaluative component directly informs the needs assessment for the next round of course development. The design team has valid and reliable information about which skills still need to be developed even after training.

Multiple inputs

There is rarely one silver bullet that solves a problem. Such is the case with needs assessment. In order to align knowledge and skills to roles and fill performance gaps to achieve business goals, data must be collected to define the business need and define the skill deficits that should link to improved individual and business performance. Data collection is often cumbersome, especially for instructional designers who tend to shy away from highly quantitative and analytical processes. When pressure to meet timelines is added to an under-staffed team with limited resources, the analytical aspects of needs assessment can receive short shrift. Thankfully, there are multiple ways to gather data and gain insights. Table 6.1 shows several quantitative and qualitative approaches to needs assessment.

Table 6.1 Needs assessment approaches

Approach	Target audience	Types of information/value
Key person interviews	• Business leaders • Future learners • Supervisors of future learners	• High-quality information; opportunity to probe with questions
Focus groups	• Business leaders • Future learners • Supervisors of future learners	• Multiple insights simultaneously • Wisdom of crowds • Ability to probe for additional information
Competency assessments	• Future learners • One level up and one level down	• Defines the gaps across competencies for a specific level
Needs assessment survey	• Future learners • One level up and one level down	• Efficient way to gather quantitative and qualitative data • Easy to summarize and prioritize • Subject to bias – may not be as valid and reliable as a competency assessment
Evaluation data	• Learners opinions about the quality of the course	• Efficient way to gather quantitative and qualitative data • Easy to summarize • Provides insights about what did/did not work in training in the past
Root cause analysis	• Instructional design team • Stakeholders	• Gain insights by reviewing data from other needs assessment techniques • Use deductive reasoning and brainstorming to determine causes of gaps that may be hidden within the data

CASE STUDY   Needs assessment in action

In this section we will share how a professional services firm used a variety of methods during a needs assessment process prior to creating talent development programmes.

Needs assessment: multifaceted approach

Among the Big Four professional services firms, development programmes are an essential part of attracting, developing and retaining a highly skilled population of auditors, tax professionals and consultants. Each line of business has specialized curricula that begin with onboarding and continue with a levelled approach to teaching proprietary methods for serving client needs. Certain critical topics such as International Financial Reporting Standards have a specialized curriculum that is integrated throughout the firm so that all levels from associates to partners understand the principles, know how to use the tools and processes, and serve the needs of the client in accordance with industry standards and proprietary methods. This is no small feat considering each firm has more than 100,000 employees worldwide and the process of hiring and developing employees runs continuously throughout the year.

In order to stay current with new regulatory requirements, technology innovations and methodological revisions, the learning and development groups at these firms conduct needs assessments regularly. One of the firms contracted with the CEB to assist with a needs assessment. The internal measurement group at the firm had the requisite skills to conduct the needs assessment, but due to other commitments, they did not have the capacity to execute the entire process in a timely manner. The project assessed the knowledge and skills among senior staff and managers in the audit practice. These groups form the second and third major levels within the firm; the roles they serve on engagements are critical. Senior staff do the yeoman's work with regard to audit tasks like checking inventory, testing controls and assessing risks among many others. Managers oversee the engagement team, handle scope and budget issues and build constructive working relationships with the client. Employees tend to spend 3–4 years at each level before being promoted or moving out of the firm. Each year, staff and managers receive training aligned to their experience. Through training, experience, coaching, mentoring and self-study, they gain knowledge and skills. As such, the skill differentials can be vast between first and fourth years within each role.

The purpose of the needs assessment project was to quantify the knowledge and skill differences within each group and, if needed, adjust the firm's current programmes to close the gaps. The measurement group within the corporate university collaborated with CEB to create four survey instruments. A survey was created for each level, senior staff and managers, and one survey was created for supervisors of each level. The goal of each survey was to gather feedback about what each group knew and what each group could do on the job. The core survey items aligned to competency frameworks that were levelled for each group. The questions focused on how frequently skills are performed on the job and how competently the employees are performing them. Table 6.2 shows the structure of the surveys.

Table 6.2 Needs assessment survey questions by role

Role	Dimension	Question
Senior staff and managers	Frequency	How frequently do you perform these tasks?
Supervisors	Frequency	How frequently do senior staff (or managers) perform these tasks?
Senior staff and managers	Competence	I possess the necessary knowledge and skills and feel fully competent to perform these tasks well.
Supervisors	Competence	Senior staff (or managers) possess the necessary knowledge and skills and are fully competent to perform these tasks well.

Links to web-based surveys were distributed to senior staff and managers to gain self-ratings. Surveys were also sent to supervisors who provided a more objective, third-party view of on-the-job performance. Responses were collected over a two-week period; reminders were sent automatically from the system to non-respondents until data collection was cut off.

Results indicated that there were large gaps between first- and fourth-year senior staff for certain competencies and selected tasks. For many competencies, the ratings rose steadily from the first to fourth year. For others, the ratings plateaued after year two or three.

While the results from the needs assessment surveys proved valuable to the firm's measurement group and its internal L&D client, neither group was satisfied with that data alone. For them, the results were a starting point which provided a point of view – that most competencies developed over time. Using that point of view, they conducted focus groups and interviews asking why some competencies might rise over time while others plateaued.

Once the qualitative data was compiled and analysed with the survey data, the measurement group met with its stakeholders to do three things: 1) share results, 2) prioritize critical competencies that would be targeted during training, and 3) conduct root cause analysis discussions on prioritized competencies to help determine how to develop training. In this way, the measurement group facilitated the transition from Analysis to Design with the instructional design team.

Using competency assessments to find skill gaps

Table 6.1 lists a variety of approaches to conducting needs assessment. Among them, competency assessment is one of the most powerful and useful. Competency assessments ask employees (and sometimes their managers and direct reports) to rate their ability to perform tasks that align to core competencies for a job role. Ideally, the assessment has been validated against on-the-job performance. If so, the resultant scores are a good predictor of job performance. That is to say, if someone scores highly on the competency assessment, then the instrument predicts with good accuracy that the person will perform well on the job. If the person scores poorly, they are unlikely to do well on the job.

CEB Talent Assessment, formerly known as the assessment company SHL, uses the model shown in Figure 6.6 to assess competencies. Assessments gather information about a candidate's potential, readiness and fit for a job. Applicants that align on all three dimensions become leading candidates for the job.

Figure 6.6 CEB Talent Assessment's approach

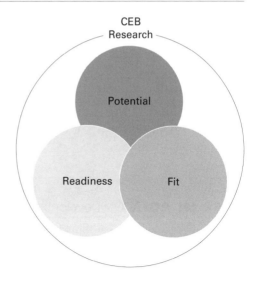

Potential
- Motivations/aspirations
- Aptitude
- Aspiration
- Work styles

Fit
- Job fit
- Network fit
- Culture fit
- Engagement

Readiness
- Work experiences
- Knowledge
- Skills
- Ability

The Occupational Personality Questionnaire (OPQ) is a personality-based assessment that can be used to measure competence. Most often, competency assessments are used for selection – to identify the best potential employee for a job among a large pool of candidates. Recruiters rely on competency assessments to make their jobs more efficient by sifting through the chaff to find the wheat.

In addition to candidate selection for open jobs, competency assessments can be used to identify high-potentials for future leadership positions. Once high-potentials are identified, their assessments are reviewed to determine areas of opportunity so they can enrol in learning programmes or take on stretch assignments to fill gaps.

In the two assessment situations mentioned above – employee selection and high-potential identification – the goal is to identify one person for hiring (selection) or a small number of people for development and promotion (high-potential). The focus is on the individual and his or her scores. The same assessments can be used to provide a macro view of the competencies across an organization. When given to a group of employees, a competency assessment provides insight into bench strength – the skills and abilities resident among a group of employees – and insight into gaps – areas where skills and abilities are lacking. These insights are gained simply by aggregating and reporting the results at a group level.

With insights from a competency assessment, instructional designers can create programmes to address knowledge and skill gaps. Because the assessment is validated against job performance, the instructional designers can act with confidence, knowing their interventions will impact on the job skills.

CASE IN POINT   Developing a learning needs assessment for high-potential employees

CEB Talent Assessment's model for identifying high-potentials also includes two additional dimensions – development and management. Why? Isn't identification sufficient? Well, no. Research shows that organizations do not do a good job of identifying high-potentials. Typically, they rely on current performance as a leading indicator of high-potential ability. Unfortunately, only 15 per cent of high performers are actually high-potentials.[17] After high-potentials have been identified and go to training, 95 per cent of organizations fail to follow through on development plans. Learning becomes scrap and growth is not optimized.[18] Finally, businesses do not manage the high-potential process well, and as such, 73 per cent cannot show business outcomes or ROI for their efforts.[19] Figure 6.7 shows CEB's high-potential business process.

Figure 6.7 CEB's High Potential Business Process

Identify	**Manage**	**Develop**
Measures factors critical to HiPo success to accurately identify HiPos and benchmark your competitive positioning	Apply best practice insights and tools to manage your HiPo programme	Provides easy, efficient and scalable development with real performance impact

The three-step approach focuses on identifying high-potentials, developing them and managing a programme, rather than individuals.

Identify

Many organizations believe that high performers are also high-potentials who will transition well into leadership positions. CEB has found that the best predictor of high-potentials includes a mix of competencies that align to three dimensions:

- **Aspiration to rise to senior roles**
  Measure what motivates someone and his or her natural styles at work. Questions target the specific components of aspiration that research shows are associated with rising to senior roles.

- **Ability to be effective in more senior roles**
  Measures are collected that combine work styles and cognitive reasoning, enabling administrators to understand *preferences and ability* for analysing data.

- **Engagement to commit to the organization and remain in challenging roles**
  Engagement is assessed with an interview guide for small populations and with the Manager Online Engagement Survey for larger populations.

Figure 6.8 shows that the intersection of these three dimensions helps identify high-potential candidates. Moreover, CEB research indicates that aspiration has an 11-fold influence on achieving an executive position; ability has a 12-fold influence and engagement has a two-fold influence. As such, this tool accurately identifies high-potentials. Benchmarks are also provided across the three dimensions so organizations can prioritize development options for individuals and groups.

Figure 6.8 CEB's HiPo Identification Model

A **proven high performer** with three distinguishing attributes:

1 High Aspirations

Yields **11x** higher probability to achieve executive position. *Will they get there?*

2 High Ability

Yields **12x** higher likelihood of being effective in senior roles. *Will they be effective?*

3 High Engagement

Yields **2x** higher probability to stay, put in extra effort and meet performance goals. *Will they remain with your company?*

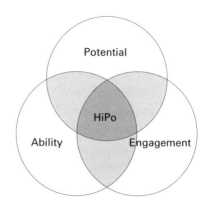

Develop

Formal learning is a critical part of development for individuals throughout their careers. Yet, the learning industry has recently begun embracing the obvious – that formal learning is becoming less influential and informal learning is gaining influence on performance. This is especially true for leaders, where the competencies, knowledge and skills that need to be acquired are far less technical and are often difficult to teach in the classroom. Research indicates that performance improvement can jump upwards of 30 per cent if leaders are first exposed to critical experiences and then learn how to extract learning from those experiences.[20] Learning how to learn is a critical skill, and it often comes from taking time to practise what is learned, reflecting on why it worked (or did not work) and receiving feedback from a coach or mentor.

To facilitate this process, CEB has created a web-based tool called DevelopmentCoach™. This system uses the results gathered from the high-potential assessments to determine viable learning experiences to address areas for improvement. Instead of making managers and employees figure out which work experiences will be most beneficial for high-potentials, the system uses a unique algorithm to translate each person's competency scores into a prioritized list of experiences that will be most valuable for that person. For example, if three competencies – relating and networking, persuading and influencing, and leading and supervising – need improvement, a good experience would be to lead a cross-functional project that requires collaboration from many teams/groups with competing goals and priorities. The output from the DevelopmentCoach™ system is an action roadmap of experiences that the high-potential should undertake to build competencies for future roles. Development occurs during each experience, but the system also tracks statements from the high-potential. It gathers information about what was learned. It gathers the learner's reflections on learning and performance, and then it invites a coach to provide feedback as well. The process is iterative with each experience so that the practice-reflection-feedback cycle reinforces development.

Manage

In order to manage the high-potential process, CEB recommends participating in CEB's Learning and Development Leadership Council and applying the best practices from it. Additionally, the management process is more than just identifying the high-potentials. Management entails seeing the high-potential programme as a three-step process: Identify, Develop and Manage. Adhering to the entire process should ensure that high-potentials thrive and eventually influence business outcomes and provide an ROI.

Conclusion

One of the best ways to ensure that training aligns to business needs is to first analyse the performance gaps in the organization that relate to the business needs. The second step is to assess whether the capabilities of the workforce are a factor in the performance gaps. When an L&D group conducts a needs assessment well, it helps create programmes that develop talent throughout the organizations. When needs assessment is conducted poorly, there are negative time, cost and performance implications for the organization. See Figure 6.9 for several examples of negative consequences.[21]

When developing training, instructional designers often rely on the ADDIE model. The first step, Analyse, is heavily focused on determining business needs and knowledge and skill gaps that align with those needs. The needs assessment process may use methods such as opinion-based surveys, focus groups, interviews and competency assessments to gather data about gaps. This chapter shared examples of opinion-based surveys and competency assessments as ways of

Figure 6.9 Consequences of poor needs analysis

Poor needs analysis leads to inefficient use of time, higher costs and performance issues.

Time and cost implications	More learner time spent attending irrelevant learning solutions
	More time spent by learners after the learning intervention in trying to understand how to apply the learning
	More time spent by managers in trying to support learners in understanding how to apply the learning
	More time spent by L&D developing programme content, as programme focus is not effectively targeted
	More time spent by L&D after the learning intervention supporting learners who struggle to apply learning
	More time spent by L&D educating learners attending programmes irrelevant to their needs
	More money spent on unnecessary learning solutions
Performance impact implications	Poor application translates into individual performance challenges which translate into wider business performance problems

defining gaps. It also emphasized that the last phase of the ADDIE model, Evaluation, provides valuable input for the next iteration of development programmes. Evaluation results indicate whether programmes are effective and how they can be improved to close gaps.

Endnotes

1 Diane Valenti (2014) 4 questions to align training with strategic objectives, Association for Talent Development, 27 May [online] https://www.td.org/Publications/Blogs/L-and-D-Blog/2014/05/4-Questions-to-Align-Training-with-Strategic-Objectives.

2 Jay Bahlis (2014) Maximize training impact by aligning to business goals, whitepaper, BNH Expert Software, Inc [online] http://www.bnhexpertsoft.com/english/resources/salt06.pdf.

3 David L Vance (2010) *The Business of Learning: How to manage corporate training to improve your bottom line*, Poudre River Press, Windsor, CO, p 130.

4 David L Vance and John Mattox II (2015) Building a framework for what matters in HR, ReimagineHR Symposium, Chicago, CEB, October.

5 Instructional Design Central (2015) *Instructional Design Models* [online] http://www.instructionaldesigncentral.com/htm/IDC_instructionaldesignmodels.htm.

6 8 Robert K Branson, Gail T Rayner, J Lamarr Cox, John P Furman, F J King and Wallace H Hannum (1975) *Interservice Procedures for Instructional Systems Development* (5 vols) TRADOC (Pam 350–30) Ft Monroe, VA: US Army Training and Doctrine Command, August 1975.

7 Outsource 2 India (2015) The ADDIE Instructional Design Model [online] https://www.outsource2india.com/LearningSolutions/articles/ADDIE.asp.

9 Walter Dick and Lou Carey (1978) *The Systematic Design of Instruction*, Harper Collins College Publishers, New York.

10 Allison Rossett (1987) *Training Needs Assessment*, Educational Technology Publications, Englewood Cliffs, NJ, p 62.

11 12 US Office of Personnel Management (2016) Training and development: planning and evaluation–training needs assessment [online] https://www.opm.gov/policy-data-oversight/training-and-development/planning-evaluating/.

13 John Mattox II (2011) ROI: The report of my death is an exaggeration, *T+D Magazine* [online] https://www.td.org/Publications/Magazines/TD/TD-Archive/2011/08/ROI-the-Report-of-My-Death-Is-An-Exaggeration.

14 Peter Rossi and Howard Freeman (1993) *Evaluation: A Systematic Approach*, 2nd edn, Sage Publications, Newbury Park, CA.

15 Nick Bontis (2009) The Predictive Learning Impact Model, whitepaper, KnowledgeAdvisors, Chicago, IL.

16 CEB (2009) Refocusing L&D on business results: bridging the gap between learning and performance, CEB Learning and Development Leadership Council, internal CEB report.

17 CEB (2010) Corporate Leadership Council, The disengaged star: four imperatives to reengage high-potential employees, internal CEB report.

18 CEB (2013) Corporate Leadership Council, Succession strategies for the new work environment, internal CEB report.

19 20 CEB (2012) Corporate Leadership Council, HiPo programme operations and outcomes survey, internal CEB report.

21 CEB (2011) CEB Learning and Development Leadership Council, Rethinking needs analysis: managing the demand and supply of learning, internal CEB report.

Access to the CEB resources cited in this book is limited to members. For information about membership, please contact CEB's Member Support Centre at CEB.Support@cebglobal.com or +1-866-913-2632.

Benchmarks 07

A journey of a thousand miles begins with one step

Measurement is a journey. Sometimes the measurement journey begins with a visionary leader who sees the value of measuring, monitoring and continuously improving processes. Sometimes it grows organically as a grass-roots effort among professionals interested in demonstrating the value of their work. Sometimes it begins because a new law mandates change. Regardless of how it starts, the journey can be long and have many turns. Sometimes there are potholes, bridges and hairpin turns along the way. This chapter will help you build a road map that begins with a measurement framework and ends with standards for reporting results.

Thankfully, guidance is available along the way. Carnegie Mellon University provides one map in the form of a Capability Maturity Model.[1] It describes a framework designed to help develop and maintain software. CEB has adopted the model and modified it to describe the maturity curve associated with implementing and maintaining measurement processes within the learning and develop arena.

Each of the five levels in the framework describes a maturity milestone. Level one is the first milestone along the journey. At this level, organizations intend to evaluate programmes, but very little measurement actually occurs. Measurement efforts are not systematic and certainly not strategic. At best, efforts are tactical. Evaluation and testing processes are not consistent. Level two is reached when tactical processes become consistent, replicable and efficient. At the third level, the analytic processes are comprehensive and standardized. Measurement becomes strategic at the fourth level when collection, reporting and decision making are integrated into existing business processes. The highest level involves joining disparate data sets and helping leadership gain insights across business processes. Figure 7.1 provides a graphic description of CEB's Measurement Maturity Model for learning and development.

Figure 7.1 CEB's Measurement Maturity Model

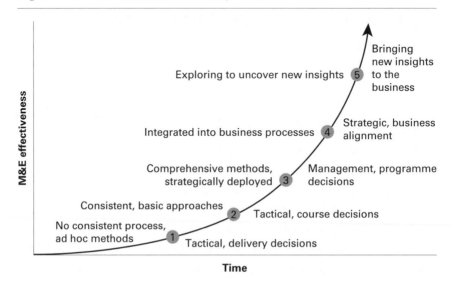

Many factors contribute to the successful development of a measurement strategy and the execution of effective measurement processes. Among those factors, leadership and governance are most critical. Without leadership support, most measurement efforts fail to gain traction and do not receive the resources required to build sustainable processes. Other factors that play a critical role in growing maturity within organizations include: the use of standard measurement tools like SmartSheets (Chapter 3), establishing a measurement team (or at least a full-time measurement leader), deploying the right technology to make the measurement processes efficient and scalable, and leveraging best practices to gather, analyse, store and report data. All of these efforts help organizations build sustainable processes to advance up the curve as well as maintain a stronghold at a given level.

Benchmarking improves maturity

One valuable activity for increasing the maturity of measurement processes is benchmarking – or the ability to compare one's current performance to the performance of similar others. Once an organization begins measuring its performance, it can monitor key metrics and compare them to benchmarks and goals. These are critical steps in any continuous improvement process. In this way, benchmarks provide a point of reference that helps organizations improve. This chapter focuses on several aspects of benchmarking using learning analytics.

For now, let's pause our journey momentarily to investigate the origin of the term benchmark. The term bench mark (two words) comes from a physical attribute that was added to buildings during construction centuries ago. Surveyors chiselled a horizontal recess into a stone in the foundation. Into that stone an angle-iron could be fitted to form a 'bench' for the accurate placement of a levelling rod for future measurements.[2,3]

To distinguish the recess from other recesses on a building, an arrow was often chiselled below it. Figure 7.2 shows the bench mark, an arrow and the actual height above sea level. In addition to this traditional definition, the term bench mark is also used more broadly to indicate a verified point of elevation such as 575 feet above sea level at the top of a hill. From the bench mark, other geographical points can be measured for height.

A new bench mark is created by determining height relative to other known points. Ideally, one of the points of comparison is a fundamental bench mark, a point that is precisely known typically because of its relationship with a local sea level. In the surveying world prior to Global Positioning Systems, professional surveyors needed a clear line of sight using a transit (eg a specialized telescope) to establish a network of elevations. By observing other points and using trigonometry, they could determine the height of a given point. Global Positioning Systems use the same principles to determine elevation. Instead of line of sight, as used with bench marks, position is determined by sending radio waves to three or more satellites orbiting the earth. The angles, time and distance are automatically calculated to determine altitude.[4]

Figure 7.2 A bench mark symbol and elevation marker on a building

The Merriam-Webster dictionary indicates the primary definition of a benchmark aligns with the historical definition described above:

> A mark on a permanent object indicating elevation and serving as a reference in topographic surveys and tidal observations.[5]

The secondary definitions reflect how the term has been adopted and adapted in the English language as a one-word noun with a meaning that stretches beyond its physical characteristics:

> A point of reference from which measurements may be made; something that serves as a standard by which others may be measured or judged; a standardized problem or test that serves as a basis for evaluation or comparison (as of computer system performance).

Benchmarking is a comparison exercise driven by underlying competitive motives. You have probably witnessed such competitions starting young. Think of the boys in primary school facing each other with hands to foreheads measuring their height against each other. Somehow even the shortest still feels equal when his hand leaves his forehead and he raises it to meet his slightly taller peers!

The differences in height among a group of young boys may only be a few inches from the smallest to the tallest. Statistically, there may not be a significant difference. Yet, for the boys those few inches can have a profound impact on pecking order, qualifying for team sports and self-worth. In this chapter, we'll address the issue of statistical and substantive significance. It is an important distinction when comparing courses to internal and external benchmarks. The right comparison and the right interpretation can mean the difference between continuing a programme or ending it. It could mean funding or not funding a new initiative. We will provide guidance that should help you interpret comparisons to benchmarks in a way that will provide maximum insight.

In the business world, benchmarking is a comparison process. Often business leaders ask, 'How efficient are our competitors' processes?' and 'How profitable are their products?' Once the benchmarks are known, they are compared to internal measures to determine overperformance (performing better than the benchmark) or underperformance (performing worse than the benchmark). Overperformance typically leads to a continuation of the 'as is' state. Underperformance often leads to a continuous improvement process like Six Sigma[6] to help identify broken processes, implement change and improve performance.

Why are benchmarks valuable in the L&D space?

Benchmarks are valuable for learning and development departments for the same reasons they are valuable in other arenas. They provide:

- a point of comparison (internal and external across industries) for current processes;
- a point of comparison (primarily external) for establishing new processes;
- context in a broader landscape (by comparing across many other industries – eg we know that scrap is lowest among retail clients) for goal setting and world-class performance;
- inputs to a continuous improvement cycle.

What benchmarks are available?

Before answering the question 'What benchmarks are available?' it is worthwhile to investigate 'What benchmarks should we collect?' With the proliferation of data in general (eg Big Data), it is clear that the volume of data is not the issue. In Nate Silver's words, the issue is to find the signal within the noise.[7] In other words, what are the meaningful metrics that should be gathered to evaluate learning and development programmes and are they good indicators of performance? Chapter 8 will answer this question with a definitive perspective. It explains that organizations should use Talent Development Reporting Principles (TDRp). That framework recommends collecting data in three categories in order to create a comprehensive report about L&D's efforts: Efficiency, Effectiveness, Outcomes. (See Chapter 2 for detailed definitions.)

- Efficiency measures in the L&D space focus on the number of programmes delivered, the way they were delivered (eg instructor-led vs virtual vs self-paced, etc), the number of people who attended and the cost of training.

- Effectiveness measures assess the quality of training usually in line with the models developed by Kirkpatrick, Phillips, Bersin, Brinkerhoff or Hale (discussed in Chapter 2). Measures typically determine the extent to which learning occurred, how much learning will be applied and how much individual and organizational performance will improve.

- Outcome measures come from business systems, typically the operations and finance tools that collect information about production, sales, costs, revenue and customer satisfaction, among others.

The availability and volume of benchmarks in these three categories vary widely. Efficiency measures for the L&D industry are readily available from the Association for Talent Development (ATD).[8] Efficiency measures can operate at different levels. Popular programme-level measures include participation and completion rates, and time spent on programme per learner. Function- or organizational-level efficiency measures can include investment efficiency metrics (eg spend per employee) and activity efficiency metrics (eg hours of programmes per employee).

Effectiveness benchmarks can be found within organizations that use standards for collecting data and reporting aggregate information. However, the most comprehensive source of L&D benchmarks for training quality is Metrics That Matter™. Since 1999 the web-hosted evaluation system has collected quality information across hundreds of corporate universities and learning providers. It houses more than a billion data points and mines the most recent three years of data when calculating benchmark values for reports. For each organization, demographic data is also collected to create four main reporting categories: industry, course type, job type and geographic location. In this way, results can be mined to create benchmarks that align closely with the attributes for a given class. For example, if Walmart were running a manager training class for high-potentials in Singapore, the benchmark could be filtered in the following way: industry – retail; course type – executive development; job type – manager; and geography – South East Asia. The ability to drill deeply into the benchmark increases the relevance of the comparison. As more filters are applied to increase a benchmark's relevance, one must be careful that the size of the comparison group remains robust. Other tools like learning management systems and web-based survey tools gather effectiveness data in large quantities, but few if any ask a core set of standard questions to create a database of benchmarkable information that encompasses many organizations.

The MTM system allows organizations to benchmark internally as well as externally. The benchmark value is the average score across all organizations that align to the demographic criteria (eg retail, executive development, manager and South East Asia). MTM has also created benchmarks for the top 25 per cent and top 5 per cent of all learning programmes, allowing users to compute benchmarks and set strategic goals using stricter performance scores.

Outcome benchmarks are much more difficult to collect and report because outcomes are measured in so many ways across organizations. Even common measures like revenue, which should have standard definitions, are calculated in a variety of ways across organizations. When consistent measures are gathered, benchmarks can be created. Other measures like customer satisfaction vary in the way they are collected (eg 5-point scale vs 7-point scale; different questions across companies; different target samples), making comparability difficult. Until standard measures are defined, such as Net Promoter Score, EBITA (earnings before interest, taxes and amortization), profitability margin, etc, and gathered using consistent methods, it will be nearly impossible to create a database of comparable outcomes.

As part of the TDRp initiative, efforts were made to collect standard outcome measures with the intent of creating a database for comparison. Table 7.1 displays some of the benchmarks from a preliminary TDRp data set. This table provides benchmarks for three measures: revenue, customer satisfaction and employee engagement. The columns labelled 'Count' reflect the number of organizations that contribute to the measure for each industry. Notably, some measures have only one organization contributing results and many have none, reinforcing the reality that it is often difficult to collect and report outcome data from a large number of businesses.

Because it is difficult for L&D to gather business outcome benchmarks, CEB recommends relying on the benchmarks that other industry leaders collect. The American Productivity and Quality Council (APQC) offers a comprehensive set of benchmarks that supplies a good set of outcome measures.[9] Their Open Standards Benchmarking Database contains data in the following functional areas:

- financial management;
- human capital management;
- information technology;
- innovation;
- product development;
- sales and marketing;
- supply chain management.

The value of using an external vendor for benchmarks is substantial. First, they have access to information that is not available to most L&D departments. Second, they undertake the time and effort

Table 7.1 Outcome measures

Industry	Revenue (average)	Count	Customer satisfaction score (top 2 boxes)	Count	Employee engagement score (top 2 boxes)	Count
Banks	$8,466,131,250	4				
Chemicals	$2,611,200,000	1				
Construction and materials	$222,325,000	2				
Financial services	$5,752,813,214	7	87%	1	80%	2
Food and beverage	$2,000,000,000	1			61%	1
Government and not-for-profit	$212,090,000	2	86%	1	74%	1
Health care	$2,486,825,167	12				
Industrial goods and services	$4,222,655,396	18	77%	1	75%	3
Insurance	$6,291,444,444	9	34%	1	64%	1
Media	$525,000,000	1				
Oil and gas	$4,601,250,000	1			65%	1
Personal and household goods	$10,891,000,000	2			63%	1
Real estate						
Retail	$7,875,000,000	2				
Technology	$3,274,730,833	12	93%	1	93%	1
Telecommunications	$7,004,850,000	5	66%	2	79%	1
Travel and leisure	$3,586,702,839	2	62%	1		
Utilities	$1,959,000,000	2			67%	1

required to gather, consolidate, analyse and report data in a valid and reliable way – efforts that most L&D departments are not staffed to undertake.

Benchmarks and statistical significance

When presenting results to stakeholders, a question that is often asked is, 'Are the results statistically significant?' It is a valid question and one that is grounded in the science of probability. Many professionals with undergraduate and graduate degrees have been exposed to probabilities and statistical testing. A common takeaway is that a statistically significant result is a de facto meaningful result. This is not always the case. The question about significance is often well-intended – to determine if results are truly meaningful. However, significance testing is often misunderstood and misused to the point that it can short-circuit useful conversations about the data, context and causal factors. Worse, this one question can derail decision making by driving leaders to discount relevant, evidence-based information and instead make decisions based on gut feelings. In order to avoid misusing the question about significance, let's examine why and how we test for significance.

Why test? There are typically two reasons to test for statistical significance: to determine if:

- two or more variables are related to each other (eg they covary);
- there are differences between groups (eg finance vs operations or location 1 vs 2).

Relationship testing

The simplest form of relationship testing with parametric data (continuous data like test scores, Likert scale survey responses, sales figures, etc) is to conduct a correlation analysis. There are several types of correlation analysis (Pearson, Spearman, point-biserial, etc), but they all analyse the changes in one variable as another changes. If X increases, what happens to Y? The best graphic depiction of a two-variable relationship is a scatter plot. Consider the relationship between classroom scores in secondary school (aka grade point average or GPA) and nationally normed college entrance exams (eg ACT, SAT, A-level exams). With GPA scores on the X-axis and exam scores on the Y-axis, we expect a positive relationship. As GPA increases, exam scores also increase. A perfect positive relationship would look like a straight line from bottom left to upper right. A negative relationship shows a decrease in Y as X increases. As a practical example, consider fatigue and driving. As fatigue increases, a person's ability to focus on critical driving tasks decreases. A scatter plot of this relationship would start in the upper left and fall to the lower right. Sometimes there is no relationship between two variables. In this case, the scatter plot of scores is evenly distributed across the chart.

Infrequently, there is a curvilinear relationship between two variables. For example, consider performance of on-the-job tasks after too much or too little caffeine (or alcohol). When too little or too much caffeine (or alcohol) is imbibed, performance is low. Peak performance has a sweet spot in the mid-dosage range. All of these relationships are depicted in Figure 7.3.

Figure 7.3 Relationships as scatterplots

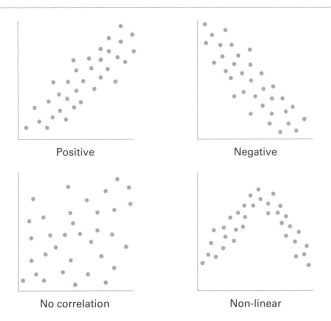

| Positive | Negative |

| No correlation | Non-linear |

To test for a statistically significant relationship between two variables, a correlation coefficient is computed, typically known as Pearson's Product Moment Correlation or, more simply, r. The r value has two characteristics: magnitude and valence. Magnitude describes the strength of the relationship and valence describes its direction as positive or negative. The r value ranges from –1.00 to +1.00. Magnitude increases as the value gets closer to –1.00 or +1.00. As the score gets close to zero, the magnitude of the relationship decreases. The significance test examines whether the magnitude of the relation is different from zero. The more extreme the relationship in the positive or negative direction, the greater the probability that the relationship is factual and not due to random variation among the data.

There is also a statistical approach for determining relationships for a slightly different set of data. If the data for GPA is changed slightly from continuous data (eg 1.0–4.0) to dichotomous data (low and high), the results would look somewhat different. The data will cluster at two points on the X-axis (low and high) and spread vertically on the Y-axis. Because the GPA scores are no longer continuous, a different correlation is calculated called the Spearman's Rho. The letter r is used again to represent the correlation and the same attributes of magnitude and valence apply. Figure 7.4 shows the scatter plots of the data we just described.

Figure 7.4 Scatterplots of continuous and dichotomous relationships

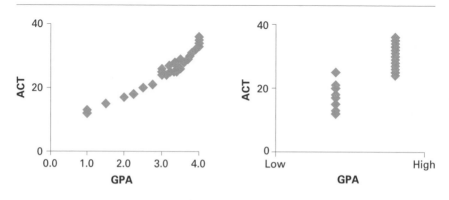

Intuition confirmed by science

When reviewing a scatter plot, it is often easy to discern if there is a relationship. A perfect positive relationship would show all dots along a single line moving from bottom left to upper right. A negative relationship would be a straight line from top left to bottom right. No relationship is represented by a random distribution of dots. Most relationships are somewhere between a straight line and no correlation – see the positive and negative scatter plots in Figure 7.3. The computation of a correlation and subsequent statistical testing for significance is designed to quantify the relationship with a single value (r), and eliminate any guesswork when the relationship has a wide spread and a relationship may not be apparent. In this way, by combining graphs and statistical testing, intuition ('I think there is a relationship') can be confirmed by probability testing.

Group differences

The second type of significance testing examines the differences between two or more groups. Statistical techniques such as t-tests and analysis of variance (ANOVA) are used to determine significance. Consider two groups of learners who have taken the same onboarding course. One group consists of experienced engineers and the other new college graduates. The course is designed to teach proprietary engineering methods that are unique to the organization. The design team guesses that both groups will gain the same amount of new knowledge and skills from training. They use a simple question on the post-course evaluation as the key metric – 'I gained new knowledge and skills from training' – using a five-point Likert scale where 1 = strongly disagree and 5 = strongly agree.

Figure 7.5 shows the survey results for this question. The average score for the experienced group is 4.50 and the score for the new graduates is 4.60. These scores suggest that the new graduates gained more from the course than the experienced group. The design team must decide if the difference is statistically significant. If so, they might decide to revamp the course or run a separate class for each group of learners.

The two distributions in the top half of Figure 7.5 overlap some-what. When there is a large amount of overlap like this, the groups do not appear different. In this case, we would conclude that the scores are essentially the same. Training is equally effective for both groups of learners.

The bottom half of the graph shows a somewhat different story. The average scores are the same, but the distributions spread less. As such, they do not overlap, and we would conclude that the dif-ference is statistically significant. Our conclusions are based on the observed data. A statistical analysis of the same data using a t-test or a one-way ANOVA would likely produce the same results. That is, for the top graph, the probability is high that the top two distributions are the same and for the bottom graph the probability is high that the two distributions are different. The distribution matters substan-tially when determining statistical significance. For the first graph in Figure 7.5, the design team would decide not to change the course or separate the learners, but they might for the second graph.

Figure 7.5 Group averages and distributions for knowledge and skill gain

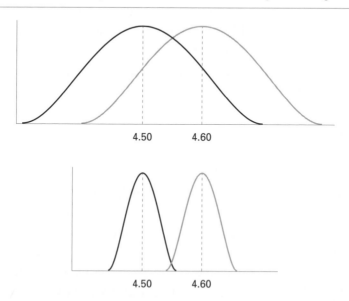

How does this relate to benchmarks?

Let's get back to benchmarks. A benchmark appears to represent a single average value, but in fact, it comprises an entire distribution of numbers. Some benchmarks are based on a small number of responses (eg N = 20) and the distribution resembles a normal curve. When the benchmark is based on a large sample (eg N = 1,000 or more), the Law of Large Numbers applies and the distribution changes shape. The average score stays the same, but the spread of the distribution shrinks and the height rises. The curve 'leaps' upward; the shape is aptly named a leptokurtic curve. Figure 7.6 shows several curves which vary in shape based on the number of responses. The Law of Large Numbers indicates that the distribution will get tall and thin as the number of responses increases. The larger the sample, the taller and thinner the distribution.

Figure 7.6 Distributions vary based on the total number of responses

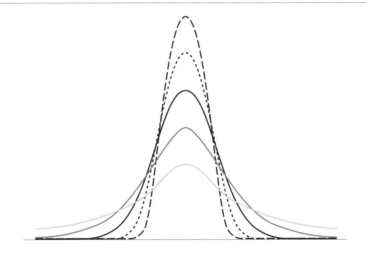

The size of the bench mark dataset has some important implications for the substantive significance of benchmark comparisons. Substantive significance means that the difference between two groups (or the relationship between them) is large enough to be meaningful. Often substantive significance coincides with statistical significance.

Sometimes it does not. Like beauty, substantive significance is often in the eye of the beholder. A small difference between the average score for a course (4.50) and the benchmark score (4.52), is not substantively different. The two values are essentially equal. However, this difference of 0.02 can be statistically significant with a large data set because the spread of the distribution gets so small that there is little or no overlap between the distributions. While a statistical analysis may indicate there is a significant difference between 4.50 and 4.52, the substantive difference is meaningless because the values are essentially the same.

Practical significance

At this point, it is advisable to move away from an exclusive reliance on the science of significance testing and towards a more pragmatic approach. On a five-point scale the difference between 1 and 2, known as the interval, is equal to the interval between 4 and 5. On a five-point scale, there are four intervals: 1–2, 2–3, 3–4 and 4–5. It is important to note that theoretically there are five intervals on a five-point scale. The theoretical scale ranges from 0.5 to 5.5, and the first interval ranges from 0.5 to 1.5. Every interval has a range of 1.0. The last interval is 4.5 to 5.5. In the real world, we never observe values less than 1 or greater than 5. For this reason, we have taken a more practical approach to intervals. With only four intervals, each accounts for 25 per cent of the scale. If two distributions differed by one full point, the difference would represent a 25 per cent difference. Even with a small sample, a large difference like 25 per cent is likely to be statistically significant. More importantly, a 25 per cent difference is a meaningful difference.

Determining the threshold of practical significance for a particular metric is challenging and requires substantial knowledge of what is being measured. A 20 per cent difference might be large, and a 5 per cent difference might not be. The threshold for practical significance must be determined by the L&D function with input from stakeholders. For some groups a 5 per cent difference is important. For others the difference is not meaningful until it reaches 10, 15, or even 20 per cent.

What does MTM bring to the market beyond benchmarks?

Benchmarks provide users with valuable information for comparison. A system like Metrics That Matter™ is able to produce benchmarks because it was designed to be a business intelligence tool. Chapter 3 describes how MTM does the following things: collect data, store and code it, analyse and process it, report it (including benchmarks) and prescribe recommendations.

Currently, many systems are able to execute on most of these steps. Data collection tools are built into most learning management systems and stand-alone, web-based survey tools make it easy to collect post-course evaluation information for courses. Yet, most tools lack the infrastructure to create long-term databases with the capacity for massive volumes of data that are categorized for easy storage and reporting. And benchmarking is only possible when standard surveys are used and data is categorized by key demographic features. Even when organizations apply standards and leverage tools like a learning management system or talent management system, their benchmarks are limited to the internal data sets they collect. They do not collect comparable external data.

The ability to collect data quickly using global, web-based survey tools has become commoditized. Free (or low-priced) tools indicate that the market has matured. However, MTM creates value in the marketplace because it not only analyses data quickly and provides benchmarks across industry, course type, job type and location, but it also provides powerful support for extracting insights from the data. Those insights start with valid and reliable instruments, SmartSheets, which are also difficult to create and maintain in this industry. Features such as Instant Insights™ (described in Chapter 3) provide real-time insight and recommended actions. In this way, MTM serves as a business intelligence tool, not just a survey platform.

How do clients use benchmarks to support decision making?

The two main reasons to evaluate training are to determine the effectiveness of the courses and to gather information to improve future iterations. Organizations that have effective evaluation processes provide leaders with summary data from the bottom of the curriculum to the top. Summary information often takes the form of dashboards or scorecards that aggregate classes into courses and courses into curricula. With an aggregate overview, L&D leaders can monitor and manage the entire curriculum. By sorting the courses within a curriculum by a set of KPIs (eg learning effectiveness or scrap or worthwhile investment), leaders can see which courses should receive reinvestment because they are successful, which should be left alone, and which should be revised or retired. Benchmarks supplement this process by providing a threshold for minimum performance.

Here is a case in point. A programme leader at an international hotel company wanted to revise a core general manager programme. The instructional design team believed it could make the course more effective by revising certain aspects of the programme. The estimated costs in terms of time and effort were substantial. When the design team pitched the revision request to the director, the first thing she did was consult the evaluation data. The course was doing quite well, scoring far above the benchmark for the hospitality and leisure industry. Moreover, the course ranked among the top programmes throughout the corporate university. The director approved neither the time nor the budget to revise the course. The course did not merit revisions and the scarce design resources were needed elsewhere to solve problems with other underperforming courses. Just by comparing results within the curriculum and against benchmarks, the director made an informed decision that saved money without impacting the quality of the curriculum.

Conclusion

Traditional bench marks (two words) are insignias on buildings that provide builders with a level platform from which they can make accurate measurements. It is also a term used to establish a reliable elevation above sea level. The business world has adopted the term benchmark (one word) to serve as a point of reference. Businesses compare their performance to a benchmark to determine over- or underachievement. The benchmarks can also be used for goal setting.

When using benchmarks, we recommend testing the comparisons for statistical and substantive significance. Be attuned to the difference. Statistical significance does not always mean there is a substantive difference, especially when large data sets are involved.

We recommend measuring the performance of L&D functions using three groups of measures: efficiency, effectiveness and outcomes. More information about measuring and reporting results using these three types of measures and their benchmarks is available in Chapter 8.

Endnotes

1 Mark C Paulk, Bill Curtis, Mary Beth Chrissis and Charles V Weber (1993) Capability maturity model for software, version 1.1. technical report, CMU / SEI-93-TR-024, ESC-TR-93-177, Carnegie Mellon University [online] http://www.sei.cmu.edu/reports/93tr024.pdf.

2 Margaret Rouse (nd) Definition of benchmark, TechTarget [online] http://searchcio.techtarget.com/definition/benchmark.

3 Benchmark (surveying), Wikipedia [online] https://en.wikipedia.org/wiki/Benchmark_%28surveying%29.

4 Figure adapted from photo of a surveyor's benchmark [online] http://www.diversed.fsnet.co.uk/os1.jpg.

5 Merriam-Webster Dictionary (2016) Benchmark definition [online] http://www.merriam-webster.com/dictionary/benchmark.

6 Pete Pande and Larry Holpp (2002) *What is Six Sigma?* McGraw-Hill, New York, NY.

7 Nate Silver (2012) *The Signal and the Noise: Why so many predictions fail – but some don't*, Penguin, New York, NY.

8 Association for Talent Development (2014) *2014 State of the Industry Report*, ATD.

9 American Productivity and Quality Council (nd) APQC's benchmarking portal [online] https://www.apqc.org/benchmarking-portal/learn-more.

Access to the CEB resources cited in this book is limited to members. For information about membership, please contact CEB's Member Support Centre at CEB.Support@cebglobal.com or +1-866-913-2632.

Optimizing investments in learning 08

Learning and development groups struggle to create value

Imagine for a moment that you are a manager of a business analytics group in your industry-leading organization. Your group is gaining substantial attention because business leaders are becoming more and more interested in the metrics that show success within the organization. Your group has even begun to link data from disparate data systems and has applied predictive analytics equations. Your most successful project provided recommendations to the chief marketing officer (CMO) about the effective use of connectors and mavens in her recent social media campaign. You demonstrated that these two social groups account for an uplift of 7 per cent in sales. Heretofore unknown to the CMO, this group drives more sales than anyone else. Your recommendations are being implemented to target this group during the next quarterly marketing campaign.

Recently, the learning and development department has been scrutinized by leaders, and they are turning to you for answers. The CEO and CFO want to know whether the investment in the corporate university is worthwhile. Should funds be allocated elsewhere to achieve business goals or should the C-suite continue to invest in costly formal training? Similarly, L&D leaders want to know what programmes their teams are developing and the leading indicators of effectiveness. Another group of L&D professionals – the ones who manage individual programmes – want to know whether their courses are working. Are they transferring the knowledge and skills necessary to improve on-the-job performance and influence business outcomes?

The pressures from these three stakeholder groups (C-suite, L&D leaders, L&D professionals) have just made your job more challenging. With other groups, you have had an inkling of what is important to them. Finance always focuses on debt, expenses and income. Marketing focuses on advertising expenses, reach, impressions, clicks and other activities that eventually lead to purchases. But L&D is a very different beast. You have talked to L&D leaders about their key performance indicators and measurement models. But as you reviewed them – Kirkpatrick's Four Levels of Evaluation and Phillips' ROI Methodology – your first inclination was that the measures will not resonate with business leaders. You can't put your finger on it, but you know that these are not the right measures to communicate.

You ask a friend who works for an auditing firm if there are models for reporting information in that industry. She quickly responds with Generally Accepted Accounting Principles (GAAP), Generally Accepted Auditing Standards (GAAS) and International Financial Reporting Standards (IFRS). She indicates these are frameworks for reporting financial results that are based on underlying principles of collecting, analysing and reporting results. You review them, and they have value for the industry, but you are having trouble determining how to make it work for your L&D stakeholders. After weeks of searching, reviewing and planning, you are still concerned that you won't be able to meet their information needs.

This imagined situation is not uncommon. In fact, many L&D leaders struggle with measuring and reporting key performance indicators that will effectively convey the value that L&D brings to the organization. The Phillips' ROI Methodology was developed to bridge the communication gap between L&D and business leaders by focusing on ROI as a measure that conveys value in a way that business leaders understand. This approach is valuable for individual programmes, but it is difficult to apply with scale across a large curriculum. Figure 8.1 shows the measures that learning organizations usually gather[1] and those that leaders are looking for.[2]

Figure 8.1 Measures reported to the business vs measures requested by the business

Top five L&D metrics reported to business	Top three business questions for L&D
1 Training expense per employee 2 Satisfaction with training 3 Training hours per FTE 4 External vendor expense 5 L&D cost per FTE	1 **Results:** To what degree will a learning programme improve a specific business outcome? 2 **Value:** What will be the return on the learning investment? 3 **Application:** How can we increase application of new skills on the job?

Developing a framework

Recognizing that many L&D groups struggle with effective reporting, Kent Barnett, the former CEO of KnowledgeAdvisors (now part of CEB), assembled a group of L&D thought leaders in 2010 to address this issue. The goal of the group was to develop a set of standards for collecting and reporting metrics that would convey the value of L&D immediately to stakeholders, particularly business leaders, but also leaders and managers within a corporate university. The group started with a focus on learning and a long-term mission to develop an approach that would apply across all aspects of talent. In the end, they created a framework called Talent Development Reporting Principles (TDRp). A full list of contributors and a summary of TDRp is available from the Center for Talent Reporting (www.centerfortalentreporting.org).[3] Many measurement approaches and models were considered by the group. In the end, substantial influence was provided by the following authors and their publications: van Adelsberg and Trolley (1999);[4] Fitz-enz and Davidson (2002);[5] Fitz-enz (2009);[6] Higgins (2012);[7] and Cascio and Boudreau (2008).[8]

One of the most influential ideas was the HC BRidge Framework from Boudreau and Ramstad.[9] (See *Beyond HR: The new science of human capital* to understand why BR is capitalized in BRidge). It focused on gathering three types of measures: Efficiency, Effectiveness and Impact. The model 'articulates the logical connections between decisions about talent and strategic success and organizes them so they can be applied consistently across different strategic and business situations' (p 47). These three groups of measures align to seven key questions for the business. All seven questions are provided here:

- Impact:
  - How do you intend to compete and defend?
  - How must we build, execute and protect?
- Impact/effectiveness:
  - What roles and structure must we improve?
- Effectiveness:
  - How do individuals need to behave and cooperate?
  - What characteristics must employees have collectively and individually?
- Effectiveness/efficiency:
  - What programmes and activities must we implement?
- Efficiency:
  - What resources must we acquire, and how should we allocate them?

These seven questions are broad enough to accommodate all aspects of managing human resources. They also provide clear alignment between the activities associated with HR initiatives, their effectiveness and their ultimate impact on the business. That alignment is appealing from a logical cause-and-effect perspective, but it is also necessary for leaders who need to be confident that the decisions they are making are based on an evidence-based rationale and reasonable information.

Within the L&D world, it is common for learning leaders to bring activity-based information to the table for decision making (eg measures from the left side of Table 8.1), mainly because that is the only information they can gather. When business leaders become aware

Table 8.1 Key performance measures for learning and development

Efficiency measures	Effectiveness measures	Outcome measures
Number of people trained	Satisfaction with training	Increase in customer satisfaction
Number of people trained by learning methodology (e-learning, instructor-led, virtual)	Knowledge and skills gained due to training	Increase in employee performance
Reach (percentage of people trained in the target population)	Intent to apply learning on the job	Decrease in risk
Cost of training per programme	Expectation that training will improve individual performance on the job	Decrease in costs
Cost of training per learner	Expectation that individual performance improvement will lead to organizational performance improvement	Increase in sales
Cost of training per hour	Return on expectations	Increase in revenue

of how much is being spent on learning – without any reasonable measures of effectiveness or impact – they often cut budgets for development, especially during economic downturns. Boudreau and Ramstad argue that cutting the budget may be advisable, but until other measures are brought to the table – particularly measures of effectiveness and impact – it is impossible to know if the right decision is to cut spending or reinvest.

The TDRp working group embraced the three groups of measures from the HC BRidge Framework and began tailoring those measures to the needs of L&D. Efficiency measures in L&D tend to focus on the types of training delivered, the number of people trained and the costs associated with training. Effectiveness measures focus on the extent to which training attendees learn the materials, will apply knowledge on the job and expect that application will improve their own performance and the performance of the business (eg Kirkpatrick's Four Levels of Evaluation). In the TDRp model, impact measures were renamed outcome measures; they address the influence of training on key business outcomes like customer satisfaction, sales, risk and revenue, among many others. Table 8.1 shares a small set of key performance indicators for L&D across the three types of measures.

There are many more measures for each of these three groups. The measures sometimes vary by industry or organization, but consistency is a critical aspect. Consistency allows for standard measurement processes, for comparison of data and for benchmarking within and across organizations. The Center for Talent Reporting maintains an active library of more than 600 measures (and their definitions) with the intent of sharing and standardizing measures across organizations.

Reporting measures to the business

Having the right key performance indicators is essential for L&D when attempting to demonstrate value. Knowing that the three groups of measures would cover the appropriate KPIs for organizations, the TDRp working group next focused on solving the barrier to effective communication – crafting the message and how it should be delivered. It was clear to the group that the medium and the message were interlocked. They searched for an effective approach and settled on a familiar format – financial statements – for conveying the message. Why financial statements? They are easy to read, especially among the C-suite, which is very familiar with the format. The team prescribed a few critical elements:

- the measure (eg the number of people trained);
- the metric – the nature of the data collected (eg number, monetary value, Likert scale, etc);
- the actual value from the previous fiscal year;
- the actual value planned for the coming fiscal year;

- year-to-date value;
- year-to-date value as a percentage of the planned annual value;
- forecast value;
- forecast value as a percentage of plan;
- notes – any important information that is needed to understand the values.

The Center for Talent Reporting recommends creating three separate reports to address stakeholder needs: Summary, Operations and Programme reports. The descriptions below share information about the audience that is targeted, the type of information that should be included and the cadence for reporting.

Summary report

This business-centric report is designed for senior business leaders and the C-suite, and it provides a macro view of the learning and development function. It summarizes activities and costs (efficiency), with leading indicators of success (effectiveness) and their expected influence on business measures (outcomes). The report displays the outcomes first, as these are the most important measures for the business leaders. Results should be shared quarterly.

Operations report

This report is designed for VP and senior leaders of L&D so they can monitor the activity, the spend and the expected value of L&D programmes across the curricula. Overall programme quality is typically the highest priority for this group, so effectiveness measures are presented before efficiency measures. Results should be shared monthly.

Programme report

This report is designed for L&D leaders and programme managers. It displays key measures for programmes aligned to achieve an organizational goal. This is a micro rather than a macro report, but it still includes measures of efficiency, effectiveness and outcomes. If the initiative is sufficiently important, the results from this report may even appear as a line item in the overall summary report. Programme leaders should receive this report monthly.

Examples of each type of report are shown in Figures 8.2–8.4.

In the Summary Report (Figure 8.2), business outcome data is being shared in the rows labelled 'Corporate goal or actual'. This data does not come from L&D. It comes from the operations and finance systems that track such data for the organization. L&D has simply asked for the most recent results to include in the report. The second line below each outcome measure begins 'Impact of L&D initiatives'. The results for these lines are computed in one of three ways.

A formal impact study

As mentioned in Chapter 4, the strategic, visible and costly programmes in a curriculum should be measured with a rigorous impact study. In Figure 8.2, the first metric (revenue) reflects that an impact study was conducted; results indicate that training influenced revenue by 4 per cent. This value is input into the table for the Jun YTD value. Four per cent is 80 per cent (percentage of plan) of the plan for 2015 (5 per cent).

Estimates of performance improvement

As mentioned in Chapter 4 (Figure 4.5), an alternative to conducting impact studies is to use a survey tool which estimates performance improvement using the Estimate, Isolate, Isolate and Adjust (EIIA) approach. Rather than an impact study, assume that the EIIA method was used and the predicted performance improvement value was 4 per cent. In this way, the influence of training is estimated without having to deploy a costly impact study.

Expert opinion

Sometimes, quantitative estimates cannot be gathered. Instead, expert opinions are gathered and impact is assessed in broad terms (eg low,

Figure 8.2 Example summary report (results through June)

Impact of learning and development initiatives	2014	For 2015				
	Actual	Plan	Jun YTD	Percentage of plan	Forecast	Forecast as percentage of plan
Revenue: Increase sales by 20%						
Corporate goal or actual	10%	20%	17%	85%	20%	100%
Impact of L&D initiatives: 25% contribution to goal	1%	5%	4%	80%	5%	100%
Engagement: Increase engagement score by 3 points to 69.4						
Corporate goal or actual	1 point	3 points	1.9 points	63%	3 points	100%
Impact of L&D initiatives: low impact on goal	Low	Low	Low	Below plan	Low	On plan
Safety: Reduce inquiries by 20%						
Corporate goal or actual	10%	20%	15%	75%	20%	100%
Impact of L&D initiatives: high impact on goal	Medium	High	High	On plan	High	On plan
Costs: Reduce operating expenses by 15%						
Corporate goal or actual	5%	15%	2%	13%	10%	67%
Impact of L&D initiatives: medium impact on goal	Low	Medium	Low	On plan	Low	On plan

medium and high). The second metric (Engagement) shows such information for the 'Impact of L&D initiatives'. Executives are most interested in the outcomes on the Summary Report. However, the report should also include effectiveness and efficiency measures. For simplicity, these measures were eliminated from Figure 8.2 because examples of these measures can be seen in Figure 8.3.

The Operations Report (Figure 8.3) focuses on all of the metrics that are needed for the L&D leaders to monitor and manage the L&D function throughout the year. Effectiveness measures are presented in the first section. The results are presented as percentages (typically the top 2 boxes or percentage favourable) because it is much easier to interpret percentages than Likert scale averages. Looking at row three, 'Learning', the actual percentage favourable for the last year was 78 per cent. The plan is 85 per cent and the June year-to-date value is close to the target at 80 per cent, which is 94 per cent of the plan. The forecast has been adjusted from 85 to 84 per cent, which is 99 per cent of the original plan. The Efficiency measures are a mix of percentages, sums and costs, all of which convey the activity and costs associated with the programmes that have been delivered to date

The sample Programme Report (Figure 8.4) focuses on an initiative to reduce injuries at multiple factories and was created for the programme sponsor (Swilthe, the VP of manufacturing). The outcomes indicate that training is expected to have a 'high' impact on the goal of reducing injuries by 30 per cent in 2015. The impact by June is 'high' for the learning events that have been deployed, but the actual year to date reduction in injuries is 20 per cent, which is only 67 per cent of plan. The team believes that injury reductions will increase throughout the year and the 30 per cent reduction will be achieved by year end. The efficiency measures in the remainder of the table indicate that the programme is making progress by developing and delivering Phase 2 courses. The effectiveness measures indicate that course quality is high and within striking distance for the forecast for year end.

Figure 8.3 Operations report (effectiveness and efficiency only)

	2014	For 2015				
	Actual	Plan	Jun YTD	Percentage of plan	Forecast	Forecast as percentage of plan
Revenue						
Participant feedback	80%	85%	87%	102%	85%	100%
Sponsor feedback	75%	80%	77%	96%	78%	98%
Learning	78%	85%	80%	94%	84%	99%
Application rate	61%	75%	55%	73%	60%	80%
Efficiency						
Percentage of employees reached by L&D	85%	88%	72%	82%	88%	100%
Percentage of EE's with development plan	82%	85%	84%	99%	90%	106%
Percentage of courses developed on time	73%	92%	88%	95%	90%	98%
Percentage of courses delivered on time	62%	90%	83%	93%	87%	97%
Participants in all programmes						
Total participants	109,618	147,500	67,357	46%	145,000	98%
Unique participants	40,729	45,313	36,998	82%	44,000	97%
L&D investment						
L&D expenditure	$15.8M	$20.2M	$12.0M	59%	$20.2M	100%
Opportunity cost	$3.4M	$2.9M	$1.3M	45%	$2.9M	100%
Cost reduction (internal to L&D)	$63K	$295K	$115K	39%	$325K	110%

Figure 8.4 Programme report (outcomes, effectiveness and efficiency measures included)

	2014			For 2015		
	Actual	Plan	Jun YTD	Percentage of plan	Forecast	Forecast as percentage of plan
Sponsor: Swiithe, VP of Manufacturing						
Enterprise goal: reduce injuries	12%	30%	20%	67%	30%	100%
Expected impact of learning	Medium	High	High	Below plan	High	On plan
Programmes to Reduce Injuries						
1. Deliver phase 1 courses for Factory A						
EFFECTIVENESS MEASURES						
Level 1: Participants	70%	80%	85%	106%	82%	103%
Level 1: Sponsor	75%	90%	88%	98%	88%	98%
Level 2:Test Score	86%	90%	95%	106%	92%	102%
Level 3: Application Rate	53%	65%	62%	95%	63%	97%
EFFICIENCY MEASURES						
Unique participants	452	3,000	2,800	93%	3,200	107%
Total participants	858	6,000	5,542	92%	6,300	105%
2. Develop Phase 2 Courses for Factory B						
Efficiency measure: complete by 5/30	–	3	3	100%	3	100%
Effectiveness measure: sponsor satisfaction	–	90%	90%	100%	90%	100%
3. Deliver Phase 2 Courses for Factory A						
EFFECTIVENESS MEASURES						
Level 1: Participants	–	80%	80%	100%	82%	103%
Level 1: Sponsor	–	90%	90%	100%	88%	98%
Level 2:Test score	–	90%	92%	102%	90%	100%
Level 3: Application rate	–	70%	61%	87%	65%	93%
EFFICIENCY MEASURES						
Unique participants	–	1,000	100	10%	1,100	110%
Total participants	–	3,000	284	9%	3,200	107%

Working with business leaders

When developing key performance indicators, it is essential to work with stakeholders – the business leaders who want to monitor the link between L&D efforts and business outcomes. Figure 8.5 provides recommended responsibilities for stakeholders as you collaborate to develop critical metrics.[10]

Figure 8.5 Checklist of responsibilities when selecting metrics

L&D responsibilities	Line leader responsibilities
• Identify key stakeholders across business areas the L&D function is aiming to impact. • Communicate the importance of partnering with the line during the measurement process. • Align L&D priorities with goals of business units. • Involve line partners in identifying measures of success for the most important learning interventions. • Consistently track the agreed-upon metrics and provide updates to stakeholders.	• Commit to partnership with L&D on the measurement process. • Share priorities and concerns with L&D. • Communicate thoughts on how L&D could support desired business goals. • Work with L&D to identify the measures of success for the most important learning interventions. • Elicit feedback from L&D about partnership to address questions and concerns as they arise.

Key reasons to involve line leaders
- Ensures L&D and the line share the same goals and expectations.
- Creates less debate later over L&D's decision making and prioritization.
- Drives a common understanding of what is being measured and why.
- Aligns L&D priorities to true business and organizational needs.

Continuous improvement and management approaches

So far we have discussed what *should* be measured and what *should* be reported. Now it is time to consider how this information should be used to make the business better, which leads us to the intersection of continuous improvement and proper management practices. The

American Society for Quality (ASQ) defines continuous improvement as 'the ongoing improvement of products, services or processes through incremental and breakthrough improvements'.[11]

It is a process for making things better over time. The ASQ highlights the following four-step process for continuous improvement and attributes it to the work conducted by both Deming and Shewhart: Plan, Do, Check and Act (PDCA). Six Sigma is a similar version of the continuous improvement cycle, and it consists of a five-step process called DMAIC:

- **Define** the goals of the improvement activity.

- **Measure** the existing system.

- **Analyse** the system to identify ways to eliminate the gap between the current performance of the system or process and the desired goal.

- **Improve** the system.

- **Control** the new system.[12]

The TDRp working group understood the value of continuous improvement and incorporated the HR BRidge Framework into a continuous improvement model for talent. Figure 8.6 shows the interaction among the three types of measures discussed by Boudreau and Ramstad (efficiency, effectiveness and outcomes) and surrounds those measures with a simple continuous improvement cycle. Sample measures are included in the figure. The Venn diagram overlaps between efficiency and effectiveness measures in order to convey the influence they have on each other. For example, a higher-quality development programme often requires more financial resources, making the programme less efficient. The interplay between efficiency and effectiveness measures leads to business outcomes and the achievement (hopefully) of goals.

The word 'hopefully' is intentionally added in the preceding paragraph because good management practices are intended to remove blind hope from any business process and replace it with informed action. The continuous improvement process for TDRp (or any process for that matter) will only be successful if it is managed. Each

Figure 8.6 TDRp Continuous Improvement Cycle

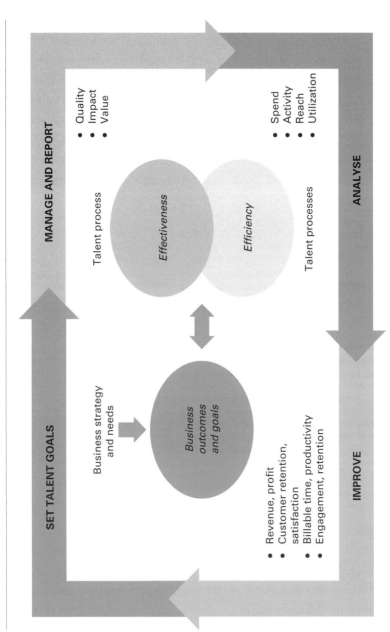

SOURCE: adapted by CEB from *Beyond HR: The new science of human capital* by Boudreau and Ramstad (2007)

step in the cycle must be executed. It seems simple, but execution is not always easy or even possible. As we've mentioned in earlier chapters, it is often difficult to define key performance indicators and subsequently gather data from appropriate sources. Additionally, it can be challenging to analyse the results. All of this is necessary before the report is generated and shared with leadership. At the Reimagine HR Summit in Chicago in October 2015, Dave Vance shared an ideal portrait of an organization that applies the TDRp approach.[13] Figure 8.7 shows the characteristics of the ideal state at the organizational level and the departmental level. At both levels, it is essential to set and agree upon goals, measure continuously, communicate regularly and hold each other accountable to the goals.

Figure 8.7 An ideal state for monitoring and managing an organization and department

Organizational level	Department level
• HR is valued, strategic business partner. • Supporting the organization's most important goals. • Partnering with goal owners and business unit leaders to help them achieve their goals. **Entails** • Proactive meetings with CEO, senior leaders. • Reaching agreement on planned initiatives and impact. • Holding each other accountable.	• HR department head manages function with business discipline — just as colleagues do in other departments. **Entails** • Creating a plan for the year with SMART goals to achieve desired improvement. • Using reports containing key HR measures to review progress against plan every month. • Taking appropriate action to get back on plan when needed.

Like effective parenting, achieving the ideal state is more easily said than done. It requires courage to have goal-setting conversations with stakeholders and to report disappointing results. Skills and partnerships are required to measure performance effectively and continuously. Monthly and quarterly meetings are often difficult to schedule and can easily be dismissed if all parties are not committed. Accountability also involves challenging conversations that require trust and cooperation in order to be successful. Many departments within a business understand and apply this management process.

It is a time-tested approach to setting and achieving goals. Technology, operations and finance departments use these principles to achieve their goals. HR and marketing departments use them less frequently. As such, the former departments tend to produce more CFOs and CEOs than the latter.

Principles

The right measures and the right reports are core to the TDRp approach. Additionally, there are guiding principles that the working group created that are worth sharing. These principles undergird the approach with rigour and provide appropriate guidelines for application. The eight principles are:

1 Executive reporting should employ concise and balanced measures that are reported in a consistent and clearly defined manner.

   a Key effectiveness, efficiency and outcome measures should be reported and tracked on a regular basis.

   b Plans should be set for key outcomes, effectiveness and efficiency measures. Performance to plan should be tracked and reported.

   c Executive reports should include, at minimum, results from last year, current year plan, current year-to-date (YTD) results and a forecast for the current year. Detailed reports typically include just the results which may be daily, weekly, monthly, quarterly or yearly.

2 Executive reports should be produced and communicated with a frequency and thoroughness to enable appropriate management of the function.

3 Executive reporting should include actionable recommendations.

4 Data integrity and completeness should be maintained.

5 Appropriate analytical methods should be employed.

6 The impact and value or benefit of initiatives and processes should be identified whenever appropriate, preferably by the stakeholder at the outset of the initiative.

7 The full costs of human capital initiatives and processes should be captured and reported whenever possible.

8 Executive reporting and the underlying databases should support continuous improvement of talent processes and programmes.

These principles provide guidance for implementing TDRp. Interestingly, as broad as they are, they may need additions or amendments in the future. For example, recent court rulings in Europe have made safe harbour laws more stringent, making it more difficult to collect data from employees across borders. This issue may already be subsumed under Principle 4, 'Data integrity' or 5, 'Appropriate analytical methods', but it may be worthwhile to add a statement about safe harbour laws and individually identifiable information to the principles in the future.

Less is more

When applying the TDRp, it is possible to become overwhelmed by the many measures that stakeholders want you to collect. As part of the first principle, the metrics team that is responsible for executive reporting should focus on the *critical* metrics. The process for gathering, analysing and reporting metrics can be time-consuming, tedious and obstructive – preventing other work from being accomplished. Adding nice-to-have metrics to the list of critical metrics can create too much burden and prevent timely reporting and use of the results. When determining critical metrics, it is essential to determine what is currently measured (and can be measured if the critical measures are not currently gathered), what the stakeholders want to monitor and what the stakeholders will be able to manage. These three levels look like a funnel from a top-down perspective or a pyramid from a bottom-up perspective. While the measures that are gathered can be larger in number, the measures that can actually be managed by leaders should be small in number.

The process for determining key performance indicators can be long and convoluted. Multiple stakeholders with multiple perspectives can make a simple task much harder. Three criteria that should be

Figure 8.8 Tips for determining key performance indicators

Relevant	High quality	Timely
• Avoid analysing data simply because of ease of collection and analysis. • Gather data that has relevance to stakeholders beyond L&D function. • Make sure data collected can be cut for specific business units, functions, or regions so strengths/weaknesses can be pinpointed.	• Provide oversight to data collection and analyses to ensure that insight is applicable to the problems it intends to address. • Keep data collection methods consistent over business units, regions and functions to ensure accurate comparisons at the functional level. • Ensure that accurate thresholds are in place to notify management when data indicates declining performance.	• Refresh data frequently, ideally whenever new training instances take place or when recurring HR processes (performance reviews, engagement surveys, etc) occur. • Ensure that ad hoc data can be collected in a timely manner, so information supporting business decisions is updated. • Keep KPIs/metrics and data collection methods consistent over time for accurate tracking of progress and improvement.

used when developing metrics are relevance, quality and timeliness. Relevance measures align to the business needs. Quality measures can be gathered consistently and are based on data that is known to have integrity. Timeliness refers to the frequency with which data is gathered, analysed and reported. Figure 8.8 displays some tips for determining the right measures for your organization.[14]

Assumptions

In addition to the eight principles, the TDRp working group articulated four assumptions about an organization that gives TDRp context and relevance:

1 The primary purpose of human capital initiatives and processes is to build organizational capability that enables the organization to achieve its goals or to achieve them more quickly or at lower cost.

2 Whenever possible, human capital initiatives and processes should be aligned strategically to the goals of the organization. HR leaders will meet proactively with stakeholders to discuss and agree on the role of the initiatives and processes in meeting the organization's goals for the initiative or process. It is understood that goal setting will involve uncertainty and will entail the use of estimates and forecasts.

3 It is understood that the business environment is characterized by significant uncertainty and yet plans must be made with the best information available. Waiting for absolute certainty and perfection is not an option.

4 The recommended reports and the underlying data will be used appropriately by competent, experienced leaders who manage the function to meet agreed-upon goals and to continuously improve.

A key message included in assumptions 2 and 3 is that uncertainty persists, even when critical metrics are defined and goals are set and benchmarked. Despite the uncertainty, the efforts to measure should continue, even if those efforts produce estimates and forecasts, rather than statistically validated results. Subsequently, leaders should include that uncertainty in their decision-making process. This assumption does not serve as a disclaimer in the event a wrong decision is made based on incomplete data. It simply recognizes that all unknowns cannot be made known and that such incompleteness in the data should not prevent appropriate efforts to bring the best available data to the table for consideration.

Moving from reporting to action

The goal of any continuous improvement effort is always to improve the focus of the effort. Looking back at the continuous improvement models mentioned earlier, they include a step for taking action (eg 'Act' in PDCA). Unfortunately, learning measurement and reporting can easily become too focused on analysis and reporting and overlook the importance of driving action. CEB research finds that actionability depends on the quality of the insights derived from the analysis of the relevant data.[15] Figure 8.9 illustrates the three primary shifts that L&D and other HR leaders must take to create analytic impact from the data they collect and report.

Figure 8.9 Shifting from analytics for reporting to analytics for impact

From HR using **data to provide talent reports**	To HR using **analytics to improve business decisions**
Purpose of reports is to provide talent information	Purpose of analytics is to improve business decisions
Information provided is driven by leader requests and data availability	Analysis and insights link explicitly to evolving business challenges
Reports provide leaders with talent metrics	Insights provide implications for business outcomes

All of these shifts are consistent with the TDRp principles cited earlier. However, making the shift can be challenging. To draw out the implications of the insights contained in L&D reports, it is critical to be able to convey those insights in a powerful way by adding a narrative (or story) to the reports. Figure 8.10 provides some guidance on the best ways to develop and communicate these types of narratives.[16]

Figure 8.10 Critical elements of data-driven story

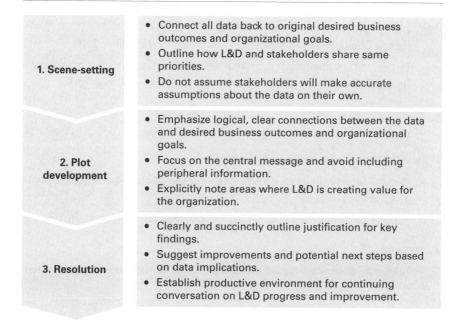

1. Scene-setting	• Connect all data back to original desired business outcomes and organizational goals. • Outline how L&D and stakeholders share same priorities. • Do not assume stakeholders will make accurate assumptions about the data on their own.
2. Plot development	• Emphasize logical, clear connections between the data and desired business outcomes and organizational goals. • Focus on the central message and avoid including peripheral information. • Explicitly note areas where L&D is creating value for the organization.
3. Resolution	• Clearly and succinctly outline justification for key findings. • Suggest improvements and potential next steps based on data implications. • Establish productive environment for continuing conversation on L&D progress and improvement.

CASE STUDY ADP learning and performance group

ADP is a global provider of cloud-based human capital management solutions that unite HR, payroll, talent, time, tax and benefits administration. The company serves more than 600,000 clients across 100 countries and has been in business for more than 65 years. ADP's mission is to power organizations with insightful solutions that drive business success.

ADP's Learning and Performance group (L&P) was an early adopter of TDRp because Carrie Beckstrom, the VP of L&P, was a key member of the TDRp working group. She is a strong believer in using standard approaches and consistent measures that lead to scalable and repeatable processes. The L&P group adopted TDRp because L&P needed to demonstrate a credible link between L&P programmes and business outcomes. TDRp offered a way of measuring the relationship between L&P activities and business outcomes.

The L&P group aligns its efforts to the needs of the business through an annual strategic planning process where the learning needs of the organization are associated with the financial goals of the entire company. Then L&P partners with stakeholders to set expectations, coordinate efforts and estimate the expected influence of training upon business outcomes. As the programmes are developed and deployed, the analytics team within L&P is responsible for measuring impact and reporting goal-based measures monthly. Here are some examples of annual goals:

- Develop associates to serve custom needs:
  - 100 per cent of associates working on large clients must complete the Human Capital Management Basic Certificate by December 2014;
  - 75 per cent of implementation and service associates must complete the Human Capital Management Intermediate Certificate by June 2015.

- Time to competency:
  - standardize onboarding so new hires achieve competency within five months.

- Improve the client learning experience:
  - monitor service requests from clients; expect a decrease in requests due to training;
  - monitor Net Promoter Score; expect an improvement in scores due to training.

- Productivity:
  - realize a 3 per cent increase in productivity across L&P with regards to their work for the company.

As the L&P group implemented TDRp, they met with barriers and successes. Barriers rose in the form of stakeholders who did not want to measure outcomes. The team also experienced difficulty gathering data once key performance indicators were selected. Successes resulted from collaboration. One of the greatest was sharing the TDRp approach with other departments and seeing their measurement practices improve along the way.

The Center for Talent Reporting interviewed Carrie Beckstrom to document the barriers her team faced at ADP. Her responses, which include recommendations for overcoming barriers, are available via a case study from the Center for Talent Report.[17] Here is one of the success stories about revenue recognition and time to competency.

While determining the key performance indicators to include in the TDRp reports, the L&P team discovered 'time to revenue recognition' as a key indicator of profitability. This time period was defined as the time from client contract signature to the time when the ADP system is fully implemented, allowing for regular billing of services. The ability to fully implement an ADP system is dependent upon the capabilities of the ADP associates on the job. More competent associates have shorter implementation times than less competent associates. By extension, the time to competency is related to the time to revenue recognition. As such, the L&P team focused on time to competency as a proxy for time to revenue recognition. L&P worked with stakeholders to identify ways to alter and improve the onboarding process to reduce (improve) the time taken for new associates to become competent at overseeing implementations. The L&P team tracked time to competency and saw a sizable reduction; by speeding up time to competency and reducing the time to revenue recognition, the L&P team estimates they saved the company $6.3 million.

Implementing TDRp is a process that requires many inputs, including support from leadership, buy-in from stakeholders, capable measurement personnel and patience. Beckstrom describes the process as iterative, similar to agile development of software, where requirements and solutions evolve through collaboration with the measurement team and business owners. Like any new process, the start-up costs of an effective learning improvement process may be high, but the returns are worth the effort. Substantial effort was required by the three-person team to implement TDRp and get it established, but once it was in place, Beckstrom estimates that the data collection, reporting and continuous improvement cycle could be maintained with one-third of a full-time-equivalent employee. Each journey is different for each company, but ADP has found success in using TDRp to monitor and manage its efforts and demonstrate value to leadership.

Conclusion

Learning and development departments struggle with their ability to show the value they contribute to the organization. Part of the difficulty is that L&D leaders do not know what to measure. At other times, they know what to measure but face barriers actually collecting the data. In the event that the L&D organization actually gathers a set of critical measures, it still faces the difficult task of communicating impact quickly and thoroughly.

Measurement and reporting frameworks, such as the Talent Development Reporting Principles, can help HR define and report the right measures. By following the framework, L&D can gather the information required to communicate effectively with stakeholders. The continuous improvement process also helps determine which investments are working and which are not. When L&D leaders effectively manage their measures, they can optimize the effectiveness of development efforts to improve individual and organizational performance.

Endnotes

1 CEB (2013) Corporate Leadership Council Analytics Survey, CEB internal report.

2 Jack Phillips and Patti Phillips (2010) How executives view learning metrics, *Chief Learning Officer* [online] http://www.clomedia.com/2010/12/03/how-executives-view-learning-metrics/.

3 Dave Vance and Peggy Parskey (2015) Introduction to talent development reporting principles (TDRp), Center for Talent Reporting [online] http://www.centerfortalentreporting.org/files/Intro_to_TDRp.pdf.

4 David van Adelsberg and Edward A Trolley (1999) *Running Training Like a Business: Delivering unmistakable value*, Berrett-Koehler Publishers, Inc, San Francisco, CA.

5 Jac Fitz-enz and Barbara Davidson (2002) *How to Measure Human Resources Management*, 3rd edn, McGraw-Hill, New York, NY.

6 Jac Fitz-enz (2009) *The ROI of Human Capital: Measuring the economic value of employee performance*, 2nd edn, AMACOM, New York.

7 Jeff Higgins (2012) *Human Capital Management Handbook*, 2nd edn, Human Capital Management Institute.

8 Wayne Cascio and John Boudreau (2008) *Investing in People: Financial impact of human resources initiatives*, FT Press, Upper Saddle River, New Jersey.

9 John Boudreau and Peter Ramstad (2007) *Beyond HR:Thenew science of human capital*, Harvard Business School Publishing, Boston, MA.

10 14 16 CEB (2014) Learning and Development Corporate Leadership Council, Playbook: measuring and communicating L&D's impact, internal CEB report.

11 American Society for Quality (2015) Continuous Improvement [online] http://asq.org/learn-about-quality/continuous-improvement/overview/overview.html.

12 Thomas Pyzdeck (2014) *The Six Sigma Handbook*, 4th edn, McGraw-Hill, New York, NY.

13 David Vance and John Mattox II (October 2015) Building a framework for measuring what matters in HR, ReimagineHR Summit 2015, CEB Conference.

15 CEB (2013) The analytics era: transforming HR's impact on the business, internal CEB report.

17 Carrie Beckstrom, Karen Bonn and Jim Abinanti (2014) ADP TDRp Case Study, Center for Talent Reporting [online] www.centerfortalentreporting.org.

Access to the CEB resources cited in this book is limited to members. For information about membership, please contact CEB's Member Support Centre at CEB.Support@cebglobal.com or +1-866-913-2632.

Beyond learning analytics to talent management analytics

09

The future is for those who can predict it

In this final chapter, we will move beyond learning analytics to examine a simple framework for understanding human resources and ways that technology and services enable organizations to leverage analytics in order to optimize and manage their investment in talent. We'll examine research about how organizations are using data and the differentiators among average organizations and leading organizations. Lastly, we'll share stories about successful organizations through case studies.

Before we begin, let's start with a bit of brain teaser. What do the following metrics have in common?

- employee blogging behaviours;
- the proportion of cars in the parking lot that are parked backwards – back-end in rather than front-end in;
- the number of Dilbert cartoons posted in cubicles around the office.

The answer is simple: these measures have been proposed as leading indicators of employee engagement. Cognizant has found that employees who blog are more engaged at work.[1] The second and third metrics are proposed measures of engagement that were shared (not validated) on Stephen Dubner's blog. If the proportion of backed-in cars is low, the organization is engaged. If the proportion is high, engagement is low, the notion being that employees cannot wait to leave and do not want to take the extra time to back out of a parking space on their way out.[2] Dilbert is an indicator of frustration with management. More Dilbert means more frustration and less engagement.[3] While the latter two measures have not been validated, they do *seem* to ring true.

Defining what to measure in talent management

Like doctors, organizations look for signs of illness – places where talent goals are not being met or where talent is not 'healthy'. And like medicine, rarely is there one cause and rarely is there one solution. For this reason, it is unreasonable to expect that one metric will sufficiently describe a symptom of illness within an organization. Certainly, the value is great if only one measure is sufficient to describe the problem, but that one measure can be limiting or even damaging if the metric is off target. A better way to approach talent measurement is to take a macro view of the entire employee lifecycle from the beginning (workforce planning, recruiting and assessing talent), through the middle (developing and engaging the workforce) to the end (transitioning through voluntary or involuntary turnover). Once the target milestones are identified for each career stage, business and HR leaders can create key performance measures to monitor and manage success. In some cases, these milestones will be different for different populations. For example, some milestones will focus on one segment of the workforce – millennials or soon-to-be retirees – and others will focus on a particular business unit or office location. The best time to define these milestones is during the strategic planning process when key business goals are defined. HR should consider how it will serve the business by answering these four talent-driven questions:

1 What are the most significant talent-related risks to achieving each business goal?

2 What talent goals need to be accomplished to avert each of these risks?

3 What metrics should we track across the employee lifecycle (and how often should they be measured) to ensure progress against talent goals?

4 What would happen if we can't measure and manage these risks and goals?

To be successful, the talent goals must be as specific as possible. Figure 9.1 shows a balanced scorecard for talent from Verizon. At the top of the figure is the Strategic perspective, which focuses on whether Verizon's people capabilities are aligned with the business needs. The Operations perspective focuses on how HR must excel to meet the business needs. The Financial perspective asks the difficult question, 'Is HR adding value to the business?' Lastly, the Customer perspective enquires about how customers (internal to Verizon) see HR.[4] Verizon collects measures within each of these four areas and reports them as their key performance metrics for HR.

Business leaders should plan to incorporate this cascade from business goals to talent goals into every annual strategic planning cycle and should examine progress against these goals in every strategic review. For some business leaders, incorporating a talent review into a business review is new. Business leaders may not be used to thinking about talent risks in the same way that they would think about financial risks or supply chain risks. But they need to begin to do so. As mentioned in the first chapter of this book, CEB's review of 500 companies that experienced significant stall points in their growth revealed that 87 per cent of the time the drivers of the stall are either partly or entirely driven by talent challenges. Only by incorporating talent risk into the business risk dashboard will organizations be able to get out in front of these challenges. Figure 9.2 provides a graphic depiction of two processes – one for leaders and one for HR – and how they integrate talent goals with business goals through integrated talent action plans. For more details about integrating business goals into talent planning and execution, see CEB's research about engaging business leaders in talent management.[5]

Next comes the hard part – gathering measures, monitoring them and managing with them. The last statement may oversimplify things a little, but at its heart, it hits the key process. Before any human capital measurement begins, HR and the business must collaborate

Figure 9.1 Talent Analytics Dashboard from Verizon

Strategic perspective

- Percentage of diversity recruitment
- Leadership bench strength

Are Verizon's people capabilities aligned with future business needs?

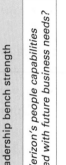

Customer perspective

- Employee services customer satisfaction index
- Benefits vendor satisfaction
- Verizon viewpoints EE Perception Average

How do customers see HR?

Operations perspective

- Cycle time-to-fill
- EE service centre operational performance index
- LRRC call volumes
- Benefits vendor operational performance
- Management placements (female and minority)

Where must HR excel to enable the business to meet its goals?

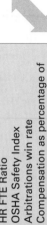

For reporting purposes, the categories only contain the most pertinent or critical measures.

Financial perspective

- HR FTE Ratio
- OSHA Safety Index
- Arbitrations win rate
- Compensation as percentage of revenue

Is HR adding financial value to the business?

SOURCE: Verizon Communications Inc

Figure 9.2 Cascade of the standard chartered process

Business
leader
output from
'SPA' session

Focused,
integrated
talent action
plans

Individual business unit-integrated
talent action plans

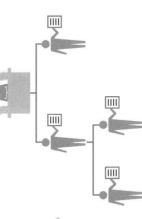

Integrated Talent Action Plan for Business Unit A

1. Increase recruiting efforts for MBA graduates
   • HR to organize campus recruitment programme
   • Leaders to allocate budget and speak at events
2. Launch leadership development programme in India
3. Develop improved sales capabilities for mid-level associates

Talent goal cascade from GM
to direct reports

Quarterly
executive
team review
of progress on
action items

HR output
from SPA
session

An HR agenda
that responds
to challenges
throughout
business units

Corporate HR agenda informed
by SPA action items

Corporate HR talent initiatives

Q1: Pilot to help managers develop
junior talent

Q2: Retention management project
to understand root causes of
attrition

Q3: Campus recruiting programme in
United Kingdom

HR resource allocation plan

• HR budget allocated to key talent
priorities for the business
• HR staff deployed to work on
the talent areas most critical for
business
• HR tools and systems supplied to
key SPA programmes for business

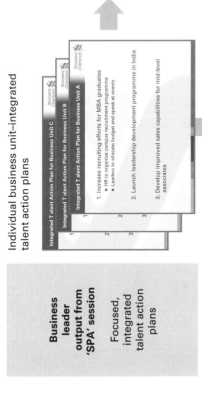

SOURCE: CEB (2008)

to determine the most important and valuable metrics that connect HR processes to corporate goals and business success. Once measures are gathered, HR is responsible for monitoring and managing HR processes that contribute to the success of the business. This management perspective as applied to learning was shared in more detail in Chapter 8 during the discussion of Talent Development Reporting Principles. While Chapter 8 focused on L&D, the principles can be applied to any talent process.

Understanding the employee lifecycle

For learning measurement to have strategic impact at the highest levels of the organization it must work in tandem with measures from across the employee lifecycle. Just as the employee lifecycle is increasingly integrated and 'always on', an organization's measurement programmes should be increasingly integrated. Later in the chapter, we will share case studies that explain how organizations have defined, measured and managed metrics to improve talent. For now, let's take a look at a framework for understanding the employee lifecycle within an organization. Figure 9.3 shows six major processes for talent management: Plan, Recruit, Assess, Develop, Engage and Perform.[6] Time and again, research shows that failures in one of these six are responsible for business derailment.

Figure 9.3 Human capital processes: Plan, Recruit, Assess, Develop, Engage and Perform

Each of the six pillars is explained in more detail here:

- **Plan**

  Establish the quantity and quality of talent needed by the organization for the next five years; determine the best strategy for sourcing talent. The planning process includes identifying the kinds of talent that will be most critical to the organization's five-year strategy, determining the quantity of talent required by role, understanding the availability of that talent in the labour market and knowing how best to compete for that talent.

- **Recruit**

  Acquire the talent the organization needs. The recruiting process includes a wide range of steps which might include defining the job, sourcing candidates, interviewing, tracking candidate quality, making a formal offer, negotiating for compensation, hiring and eventually shaking the candidate's hand as she walks through the front door for day one on the job. This process is enabled by organizational systems like applicant tracking tools and proprietary sourcing templates.

- **Assess**

  Measure the strengths and weaknesses of current and prospective employees of the organization. The assessment process, which can be used at pre-hire for incoming job seekers and at post-hire for job placement and development, involves defining critical competencies (what are they good at) and behaviours (how are they likely to act) that are required in the role and then administering tests that determine the individual's current profile relative to the required profile.

- **Develop**

  Build skills among employees. The development process is complex because it involves skill gap assessments, formal and informal training, performance appraisal, high-potential assessment, developmental planning and succession planning.

- **Engage**

  Capture the commitment and discretionary effort (minds and hearts) of employees. The engage process includes assessment, compensation, lateral moves, role and responsibility changes, secondments, promotions and eventually transition out of the organization via retirement or departure (voluntary or involuntary).

- **Perform**
  Drive the productivity of employees and their contribution to enterprise-wide results. Perhaps nothing is more complex than enabling the performance of employees across their lifecycle with the organization. This will involve a combination of management practices, incentives, work conditions, team dynamics, performance goal setting and motivational approaches.

Within each process of the employee lifecycle, massive amounts of data can be collected. Even for a small number of measures in a large company, the data sets grow quickly. To gain some perspective on the size of these data sets, it may be helpful to consider a couple of measures from three of the six processes mentioned above. For the Recruit process, two critical measures are candidate quality and quick quits. Additionally, the applicant tracking system may capture tens or hundreds of other measures. For the Develop process, two critical measures are the competency gaps across the organization and the ability to fill those gaps. These measures swim in a sea of other development measures in the learning management system and HRIS. For Engagement, two critical measures are use of discretionary time and willingness to stay. Again, these measures are part of a larger data set; the employee engagement survey may have tens or hundreds of questions. We will share some CEB research about organizations that analyse their data and manage it in a way that helps create competitive advantage. For example, organizations that can predict when candidates are likely to leave can take action to re-engage them and maintain productivity.

Interestingly, most organizations treat each HR process separately. Recruiting is different from Development which is different from Engagement. The reality is that the people being affected by the HR processes are the same individuals and as such the processes should be integrated to reflect each individual's journey through the organization – hence the interlocking circle of stages in Figure 9.3.

Integrating data

What if the data from each of these processes were integrated? Given the right data, enough time and a system that could integrate data across the processes, an organization could describe some very interesting and important facts. It could start with individuals who get hired (and those that don't). Next, performance appraisal measures or other job performance measures could be linked to hiring criteria to create a virtuous feedback loop that informs recruiting about the most and least successful candidates. Likewise, engagement scores could be integrated into the mix to determine what factors lead to long-term, highly productive employees.

Moving beyond simple statistical description, the data could also be used to create predictive models to determine who is likely to be successful, who is likely to stay more than three years and how engagement influences long-term productivity. The goal would be to gather data linking one process to another. After predictive models have been created, the organization could take action to intervene at the right times to bolster engagement, retain highly productive employees and provide development opportunities for those who are lagging. The goal of integrating data is to create an overarching theory for managing talent within each organization. That theory would align HR practices to support the business goals by measuring, monitoring and managing HR processes to ensure the right talent is in place and driving the right outcomes. Talent analytics, then, is the discovery and communication of meaningful patterns in talent data.[7]

Research on talent analytics

HR, like other areas of the business, receives constant pressure from the C-suite to perform. Performance ties back to the business objectives, and more recently, the C-suite has been pushing for better information. In fact, they want data-driven insights. A survey conducted by PwC in 2012 indicates that there is a substantial disconnect

Figure 9.4 Percentage of CEOs who believe information is important and comprehensive

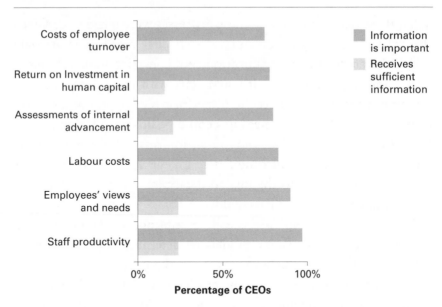

between the information that business leaders want from HR and the information that HR actually provides.[8] Figure 9.4 shows the results of the PwC study. All CEOs want information about staff productivity, but fewer than 40 per cent actually receive sufficient information on the topic. The disconnect between importance and actual information is smallest for labour costs. One would think this is a relatively easy thing to measure, but that difference is still roughly 30 per cent. Clearly, CEOs are not getting the information they need from HR. If spending projections on HR analytics are any indicator, this situation should change soon; 95 per cent of senior leaders intend to invest more in data and analytics in the next two years.[9]

The critical issue for business leaders is not lack of data. It is insight, and insights are scarce. Only 15 per cent of leaders agree that HR analytics has helped change a business decision in the past year.[10] Similarly, only 8 per cent believe they are getting significant returns for their investments in analytics.[11]

Confidence in HR's ability to provide insight is low, partly due to the lack of qualified personnel and analytic systems The situation for most organizations is very much like the farming community more than 150 years ago, prior to the invention of the mechanized reaper. Farmers could plant and grow more wheat than they could harvest. Then the reaper arrived and productivity jumped because farmers could harvest faster and more efficiently. The vast fields of data that are available for harvest today are limited by the people who have the knowledge and skills to harvest it and the systems that support analytics.

The transformation of data into insights will occur when HR makes a transition from reporting to analytics. Figure 9.5 shows on the left side the reporting processes that are typical of most HR organizations. The right side lists the activities associated with an HR organization focused on analytics. The reporting approach tends to provide information that leaders must interpret and then act upon, whereas the analytics approach provides information and insights that facilitate decision making.

As we shared in Chapter 3, an analytics organization leverages systems to allow end users to pull information; sometimes the system even performs advanced analytics and provides insights and prescriptions for action. While in-system analytics are valuable, be wary. Technology is not strategy. The transformation should include systems, but it also requires people who understand how to use the systems and apply processes that make the steps efficient and results informative.

Figure 9.5 Transitioning from reports to analytics for HR

From HR using **data to provide talent reports**	To HR using **analytics to improve business decisions**
Purpose of reports is to provide talent information	Purpose of analytics is to improve business decisions
Information provided is driven by leader requests and data availability	Analysis and insights link explicitly to evolving business challenges
Reports provide leaders with talent metrics	Insights provide implications for business outcomes

Figure 9.6 Percentage of business leaders who use HR data for key talent decisions

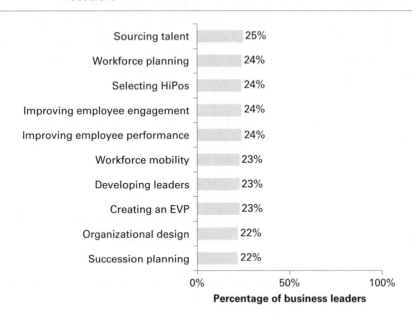

The current state of decision making for more than 9,000 respondents to a CEB survey is that most leaders are making decisions by gut instinct.[12] Figure 9.6 shows that 25 per cent or fewer of all leaders are making decisions based on talent data. Part of the issue is the maturity of the analytic systems in the HR space. As one SVP for a manufacturing company said, 'When we make our finance decisions, we use data and spreadsheets. When we make decisions about our most important asset, our people, we don't have the same tools.'[13]

The war for talent continues today as it did five, ten and fifteen years ago. Talented people are necessary to create and maintain competitive advantage; the only difference now is that better, faster systems are available to source, evaluate and track candidates. No doubt the HR technology industry is advancing. Giant technology players have acquired a range of HR and analytics companies over the past three to four years: Oracle bought PeopleSoft and Taleo; SuccessFactors purchased Plateau and then was acquired by SAP; IBM purchased SPSS and Kenexa. However, executive feedback shows that these systems are not yet producing enough insight to fully meet the information needs of the C-suite.

Jac Fitz-enz described a four-part transformation of human capital metrics that is supported by analytic systems:[14]

- transactional monitoring – human resources activity reports;

- human resources management – performance monitoring;

- business metrics – tying HR metrics to the business;

- predictive analytics – foretelling effects.

The first two steps involve gathering and reporting descriptive statistics such as the cost of new hires, the average performance scores for employees, or the employees who are capable of performing at the next level. These are essential and useful pieces of information that often get shared via static monthly reports; sometimes they are displayed with dynamic dashboards with real-time data and drill-down capabilities. The third step involves capturing business data and determining the cause-and-effect relationship between HR initiatives and business objectives. See Chapter 4 for more information on impact studies. Step four involves the application of advanced statistics to multiple and disparate data sets to create current state models based on available data and future state models with predictive equations. Common approaches include correlation, regression, analysis of variance and structural equation models; emerging techniques for HR include simulations, decision trees, random forest and various machine learning algorithms. Fitz-enz indicates that prediction is the most valuable type of measurement that can be applied.

Research by CEB has found an important paradox when it comes to implementing advanced analytics systems and building measurement groups to perform analytics.[15] At early stages of increasing sophistication, organizations receive value and benefits from implementing sophisticated analytics approaches. However, there is a point of diminishing returns, as shown in Figure 9.7. For more advanced organizations, simply having better-than-average analytics sophistication resulted in only minimal increased impact for the HR function. In other words, analytics sophistication alone is not enough to achieve significant improvements in talent outcomes.

How can we resolve the conflict between Fitz-enz's perspective that advanced analytics is extremely valuable for an organization,

Figure 9.7 Analytics sophistication produces diminishing returns

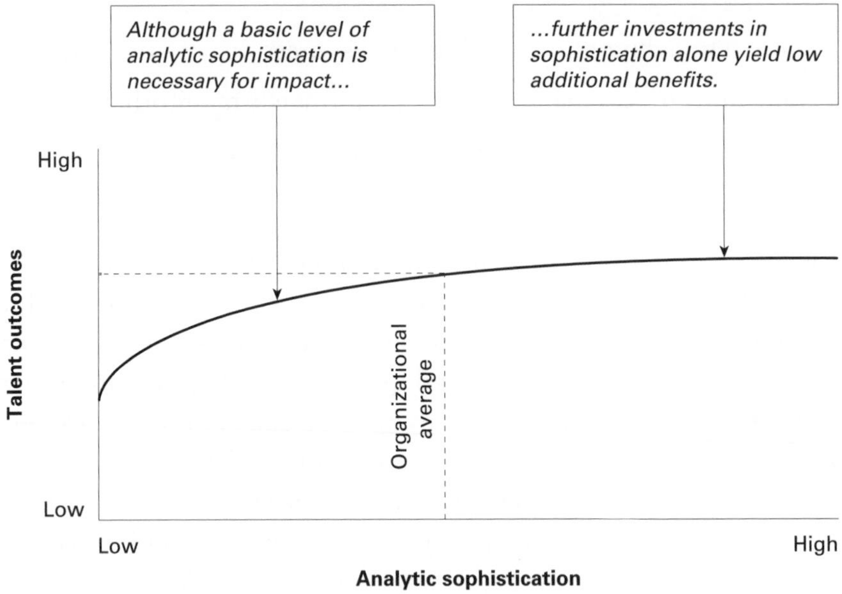

> Although a basic level of analytic sophistication is necessary for impact...

> ...further investments in sophistication alone yield low additional benefits.

High

Talent outcomes

Organizational average

Low

Low   High

Analytic sophistication

and CEB's research that shows that analytic sophistication provides limited returns? Upon looking deeper, there is actually not a conflict. CEB defines analytics sophistication in a relatively simple way with three important criteria:

- maintaining consistent data governance and standards;
- protecting data from risks to security and confidentiality;
- maintaining access systems to store data.

Fitz-enz would agree that all of these are necessary to ensure data quality and integrity. Once an organization reaches this level of sophistication, it can begin applying Fitz-enz's four steps of analytics transformation. It is necessary and valuable to create transactional monitoring and then move to performance monitoring. Before investigating cause-and-effect relationships and applying advanced statistics, it is essential to gather and report the basic descriptive information related to HR. As mentioned in Chapter 4, the effort required to do causal investigations with impact studies, and to undertake advanced statistical analysis, is substantial and costly. Therefore, a sophisticated and prudent analytics team will apply systems to make the analytics processes more efficient, but will also dedicate time and effort for customized investigations for strategic, visible and costly HR initiatives. In this way, selectively, advanced analytics can be applied to provide substantial value to the organization.

Fitz-enz also stated:

> Human resources analytics is a communication tool, first and foremost. It brings together data from disparate sources, such as surveys and operations of different units or levels, to paint a cohesive, actionable picture of current conditions and likely futures. (p 9)[16]

As a communications tool, advanced analytics is valuable, but it can be improved. Often when communicating the results of HR programmes, the value of the analysis is lost in the statistical jargon. Assuming that an analytics group can simplify its language when communicating complex analysis, half the battle is won. The other half comes from moving beyond simple understanding of the results and transforming the message into recommended actions for leaders. Analytics provides information that leaders can use to make decisions. CEB recommends that analytics groups move beyond providing results and making recommendations to sharing implications. This is where the real impact of analytics is felt. Later in this chapter, Seagate Technology is featured in a case study which shows how this organization moved from recommendations to implications as a way to build credibility with leaders. Figure 9.8 shows how the combination of decision improvement and actionable support provides greater impact for leaders.

When CEB asked for feedback from organizations that apply analytics, the results were significantly better when analytics provided both decision improvement and actionable support. Figure 9.9 shows the performance of average organizations and leading organizations across four talent metrics: bench strength, employee performance, quality of hire and employee engagement. On average, leading analytics organizations – defined as those offering decision improvement and actionable support – outperform average organizations by 12 per cent,[17] more than a full decile of advantage when it comes to getting to targets within each process.

Figure 9.8 Creating more impact from analytics

Decision improvement:

**'Analytics support from the HR
function improves talent
decisions'**

Improvement of decisions
made by:
• CEO
• Board of directors
• Business leaders
• Line managers

Actionable support:

**'HR is effective at providing
actionable data-based guidance
on key talent areas'**

Key talent areas include:
• Sourcing
• Performance evaluation
• HiPo selection
• Leadership development
• Employee engagement
• Succession planning
• Compensation and benefits

Figure 9.9 Leading analytics organizations achieve better talent outcomes

Average improvement in key talent outcomes
by leading analytic organizations = **12%**

Bench strength: 1.00 / 1.17
Employee performance: 1.00 / 1.12
Quality of hire: 1.00 / 1.10
Employee engagement: 1.00 / 1.09

Average organization
Leading analytic organizations (top quartile)

It's not the analytics that matter; it's how they are applied

CEB defines Business Application as the combination of analytics to support Decision Improvement and Actionable Support to execute decisions. Analytic sophistication is defined as effectiveness at applying complex analyses (eg higher-order data modelling and using sophisticated systems).[18] CEB research shows that business application and analytics sophistication intersect in an interesting way.

When looking at how organizations currently stand on both capabilities, CEB's survey found that only 17 per cent have analytics sophistication and apply that sophistication to reporting (top right box in Figure 9.10). A solid majority (60 per cent) of responses were low in application and low in analytic sophistication (bottom left). These organizations are just starting their measurement journey. The next largest group at 20 per cent was low in application and high in sophistication (bottom right). These organizations typically have a knowledgeable analytics group that can analyse and report almost any type of data, yet the group faces challenges like scaling analytic processes and translating results into meaningful actions for the business. The smallest group at 3 per cent was high in application but low in sophistication (top left). These organizations gather data and provide useful insights based on descriptive statistics, reported on scorecards and dashboards.

While it is nice to know the distribution of organizations across these four boxes, it is more interesting to examine the effectiveness of each group. How much do they meaningfully improve business outcomes? Application, not sophistication, is the stronger influencer here. Reflecting on earlier chapters for a moment, this finding aligns with our discussion of scrap learning. Scrap is the inverse of application. As scrap goes down, performance goes up. The analytics groups with high business application have the best results. When compared to the low sophistication and low application group (bottom left), the high application and low sophistication group (upper left) is 14 per cent more effective. This group is more effective by mastering the basics of gathering, monitoring and managing data using descriptive statistics and presenting those statistics in a way the business can readily use. The high application and high sophistication group (upper right) is 22 per cent more effective than the lower left because these organizations analyse data using advanced techniques and communicate the results in a way that has actionable meaning for stakeholders. The combination of application and sophistication leads to the greater impact on business outcomes.

Figure 9.10 The intersection of business application and analytic sophistication[9]

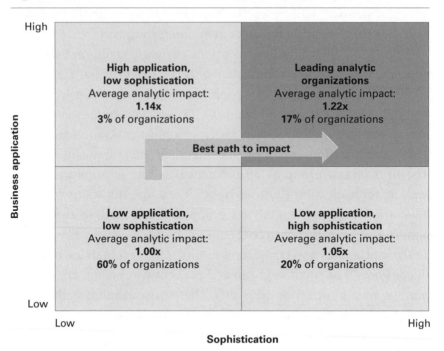

Managing data in the analytics process

There is no shortage of business metrics being collected and reported by HR organizations. Figure 9.11 shows the number of metrics tracked and reported by leading analytics organizations.[19] Interestingly, the average number in each figure (ie 81 and 49) is high. Even the lower of the two numbers (49) represents a vast amount of information to track, monitor and manage. Equally interesting is the organization that reports only one metric to the CEO or board. It brings to mind questions such as, 'Is this single metric the right metric to represent success for the entire organization?' and 'Does this metric underserve the diverse nature of the organization and the variability of metrics across business units?' As mentioned in Chapter 8, measurement systems and people are scarce resources. An HR group will be better able to manage itself when it can collect data for metrics that align directly to the business, determine which metrics are the vital few, and then spend time monitoring and managing that finite number of measures.

Figure 9.11 Measures tracked and reported to the CEO or board among leading analytic organizations

Range of metrics from leading analytic organizations

Leading analytic organizations track and report data differently than average organizations. The key difference is that leading analytics organizations have a culture of measurement. As shown in Figure 9.12, leading organizations thoroughly embrace the measurement process. They gather qualitative information that is often difficult but valuable to collect. The qualitative information often provides insight that operational data cannot. Leading organizations also establish measurement processes that gather data continuously rather than episodically. Constant data collection reinforces the culture that the metrics are important both to those who are providing them and to those who are using them. Leading organizations also standardize their measures so they can be shared and compared across business units, allowing for internal benchmarking. Additionally, if measures are standardized to industry measures, they can be compared externally. Finally, leading organizations report results throughout their hierarchy. Managers through senior leaders receive reports about the key metrics, and they receive guidance about how to monitor and manage them.

When scanning the key performance indicators that organizations choose to gather, most are common, but some measures are a little unorthodox. As we saw at the beginning of this chapter, some suggested measures are blogs, car parking behaviours and Dilbert cartoons. Compared to more standard human capital metrics, we might label these measures as 'wild'. Table 9.1 shows common or 'mild' metrics in the left column as well as unorthodox or 'wild' metrics on the right that we gathered from CEB research[20] and an article in *Harvard Business Review* titled Competing on Talent Analytics.[21] Each wild metric is explained briefly and the organization that uses it is included in parentheses.

Figure 9.12 Differences between average and leading analytic organizations

Average organizations

Exclusively tracking operational metrics

Capture operational metrics recorded in information systems, such as number of employees, performance scores, etc.

Leading analytic organizations

Tracking both operational and qualitative metrics

Capture critical talent information that is difficult to capture through traditional HRIS database fields (eg engagement and quality of hire) to expand the potential for metrics to impact business decisions.

Track broad metrics episodically

A variety of metrics are tracked at specific times across the year as they align to HR initiatives and projects.

Tracking key metrics continuously

HR identifies a set of key metrics that are measured more frequently.

Localized definitions

Metrics are measured differently across functions, business units and geographies making organization-wide comparisons difficult.

Standardized definitions

Standard definitions are enforced throughout the organization to ensure consistency and enable organization-wide comparisons.

Reporting only to senior leadership

Report findings and insights to senior leaders, such as the CEO or board of directors, limiting the potential impact of metrics.

Reporting to line managers

Report findings and insights to line managers empowering them to make decisions.

Table 9.1 Mild and wild human capital metrics

Mild metrics	Wild metrics
• Employee compensation • Number of hires • Cost per hire • Total compensation per employee • Benefit expense as a percentage of revenue • Absentee rate • Employer brand strength • Employee engagement level • Employee retention index	• Hire and promotion rate – forecast of the future organization structure based on current hiring and promotion practices (Google) • Departure probability – use employee behaviour data to identify employees who are likely to leave (Sprint) • Employee Loyalty Statistic – use a single question net promoter score to measure employee engagement (JetBlue) • Smile frequency – record the frequency with which customer-facing employees smile to determine customer satisfaction (Harrah's)

Improving analytic impact

Talent analytics is nascent compared to operational or financial analytics. Research indicates there are three common gaps in talent analytics across organizations. The first is that business leaders do not believe that HR analytics groups focus on the issues that are critical to the business; leaders believe that analytic activities are not aligned to key business measures.[22] Second, 80 per cent of senior HR leaders do not believe their groups have the requisite skills within HR to improve analytics.[23] Third, fewer than 20 per cent of HR business leaders believe that HR data is credible.[24] CEB has labelled these three gaps as issues of:

- criticality (alignment to the business);
- capability (skills);
- credibility (trust in the data).

There are viable and available solutions for all three of these gaps. Figure 9.13 links these three issues with the data that shows gaps and potential solutions. To address criticality, organizations should identify and prioritize critical measures. As shown in Figures 9.11 and 9.12, leading organizations do this – albeit, they probably gather more metrics than can be reasonably monitored and managed. For this reason, prioritization is a key aspect of the solution for criticality.

To solve the capability issue, resources should be aligned to develop the skills of HR staff to apply analytic practices. If internal resources cannot be developed, the organization can hire capable resources or outsource the analytic work to vendors. One of the critical skills to develop is business judgement – the link between HR processes and business outcomes. If HR sets goals to develop analytic skills including business judgement and HR is held accountable by leadership, the capability gap is likely to disappear to the point that it is no longer an issue.

To resolve the issue of credibility, the HR analytics team has to deliver on its promise to measure the right things in a way that ensures data integrity and also provides insight. As we discussed in Chapter 8, it is essential to have a framework for gathering and

Figure 9.13 Three challenges and three solutions for improving impact of analytics

Main issues		Solutions

1 **'Criticality'**

HR analytics is not aligned to the business needs.

'What should I measure?'

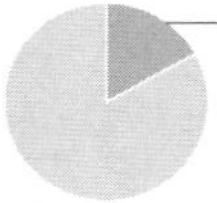

— *17% of business leaders agree*

Prioritize critical business questions

Prioritize the most scalable opportunities for business impact rather than simply fulfilling on-demand data requests.

2 **'Capability'**

Most HR leaders believe HR staff capabilities are a barrier to improving HR analytics.

'How do I upskill my team?'

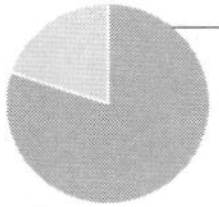

— *80% of senior HR leaders agree*

Apply business judgement to data science

Build capability in analytics and judgement; reset goals for talent analytics to focus staff on business judgement.

3 **'Credibility'**

Few business leaders find HR data credible.

'How do I increase credibility?'

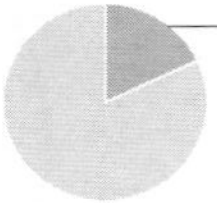

— *18% of business leaders agree*

Drive end-user ownership of talent analytics

Provide implications of decisions; don't prescribe solutions.

reporting data to leadership. Once the basic reporting components are complete, such as dashboards to show efficiency, effectiveness and outcome measures, the next step is to conduct advanced analytics with the sole purpose of providing insight. Analytics for the sake of analytics is useless. The hypotheses that are tested must align with business questions (eg is the new sales curriculum increasing sales?) and the results must be communicated in a way that leaders can understand. The communications should include insights paired with recommended actions and associated implications. By sharing implications with recommendations, leaders can weigh the options of various actions and make informed decisions.

How companies are addressing the challenge of talent analytics impact

As discussed earlier in this chapter, CEB recommends addressing the three Cs in order to use analytics to demonstrate the impact of talent solutions. These are criticality, capability and credibility.

In this section we will share how The Gap addresses the issue of Criticality, TalentNeuron addresses Capability and Seagate addresses Credibility.

CRITICALITY   The Gap's analytics prioritization principles

The Gap's centralized workforce analytics team was given a mission by leadership to drive insight and impact by aligning services to address strategic enterprise-wide needs. The team faced several challenges including diverse stakeholder needs, unique needs aligned to various brands and disparate data systems without standard aggregation plans.

The centralized workforce analytics team also had a reputational challenge to overcome. It was seen as an on-demand resource by corporate executives and HR business partners; these leaders had multiple niche requests related to their function and business interests which were not necessarily representative of larger priorities for the business. The workforce analytics team was increasingly flooded with requests such as:

- What returns are we getting from our development programme?

- What are the turnover rates for senior leaders in my business unit?

- Where can I find promotion data for the past five years?

Many of the requests were tagged 'High Importance' or 'Urgent', causing the analytics team to reprioritize often. The team was not viewed as critical to strategic analytics and decision making.

To solve the problem, The Gap had many options including hiring more staff, outsourcing the work, or implementing new technologies, to name just a few. Fortunately, leaders realized that the answer related to process and priorities. They needed to find a way to prioritize their efforts to have the biggest impact on the business. They undertook three critical steps:

- prioritize the key questions for the business;

- identify the most scalable opportunities for impact;

- create a roadmap that defines the what and how for ongoing analytics.

A critical aspect of the approach was the focus. Rather than focus on the business unit or brand level, the team focused their investments on an enterprise-wide approach that could address the most common and pressing needs across all stakeholders.

Prioritize key questions for the business

The workforce analytics team gathered data from business leaders, HR leaders and functional leaders using a survey containing 100 human capital questions. Respondents were asked to identify the 15 most important questions that would provide value to their business if the analytics team could answer them. This approach transitioned leaders away from their myopic individual needs (eg 'I need this information for my group') to broader needs (eg 'I can answer a critical business need if you provide the following information'). In this way, the approach clearly addresses the Criticality challenge by making sure that talent analytics are oriented from the beginning around what matters to the business.

Identify the most scalable opportunities for impact

After gathering the survey data, the workforce analytics team aggregated the results to determine the top 15 questions that were common across leaders. Results were prioritized from most frequently selected to least. Of course, different stakeholders wanted answers to different questions, but the results showed more consensus than the analytics team expected. In the end, the top 15 questions were selected as such by at least half of the enterprise stakeholders. In this way, they identified the most important analytic questions to drive enterprise-wide impact. Other questions that were unique to the needs of individual business units, brands and stakeholders were given secondary priority and were assigned to decentralized analytic resources. Because the top 15 questions were valued by the majority of stakeholders, it allowed the workforce analytics team to scale its impact across the organization.

Create a roadmap that defines the what and the how for ongoing analytics

The next step for the workforce analytics team was to translate the prioritized questions into metrics and clear the way for data collection, analysis and reporting – all the necessary steps to get the right inputs to answer the questions.

Once the list of the top 15 questions was defined, the workforce analytics team gathered a working team of five people, two from their workforce analytics team and three senior volunteers from the brand operations team. All members were passionate about this topic. Collectively, they set the appropriate actions for gathering, analysing and reporting the metrics associated with the top 15 questions. They addressed the following questions:

- What are the metrics associated with each question?

- Can we track the metrics or pull that data?

- What barriers prevent tracking and use of the data?

The team soon discovered they could only answer about 20 per cent of the top 15 questions with their current capabilities. So the working group got specific about what The Gap needed to invest in order to answer all 15 questions. Eventually, the workforce analytics team developed a three-year analytics roadmap based on this prioritization exercise – one that was focused on targeted, intentional investments to scale analytics to answer critical business questions.

As a result of the prioritization process and the year-over-year investments, the workforce analytics team created a dashboard for sharing results to answer business questions. Results were tracked continuously on an internal website and the team reported a near doubling of business and division use of the site since the prioritization exercise. Furthermore, business leaders have given feedback that the portal is providing exactly the information they need to support business decisions.

CAPABILITY   Building capability through talent development and analytics

The road to creating a fully capable analytics team is long and winding. While many routes are available, CEB recommends following the road that includes two critical way points: talent development and analytics.

Talent development

In order to be successful in the new data-rich, information-driven business world, organizations realize they need to develop HR staff and their ability to manage numbers and understand analytic techniques. One of the most encouraging areas of growth in HR in the past five years has been the surge in analytic capabilities among HR staff. Increasingly, HR teams are required to acquire statistical skills through university classes or online programmes. CEB provides training to HR Business Partners in the area of analytics as part of our HR Leadership Academy. We have repeatedly seen sophistication grow both in the ability to do analysis and also to provide insight through presentations, recommendations and implications.

Analytics

The ability to analyse data is critical to understanding problems and presenting solutions in data-driven organizations. HR professionals can predict the relationship between a set of employee attributes like demographics and experience, and a set of outcome measures like performance and engagement. The value of analytics is that it can often provide insights at a much faster pace than other types of analysis, such as the impact studies described in Chapter 4. Additionally, analytics can predict relationships that are harder to test through other means. A case in point is CEB's Sunstone Analytics technology that can predict job applicants' likelihood of attrition based on their résumé data alone. It uses statistical modelling techniques to analyse potentially millions of features in historical résumés for a role to identify traits that predict success in the role against a specific outcome. The approach delivers powerful (and at times unexpected) insights. For example, a top-tier strategy consulting firm found that candidates who mention interest in specific sporting activities on their résumés are more likely to succeed than those who don't.

Table 9.2 provides a representative list of answers that HR once provided for business questions (left column) and can provide now (right column) based on the available data and analytics capabilities.

Table 9.2 Answers to HR questions before and after the rise of analytic capabilities

Questions answered prior to new analytic capabilities	Questions answered post new analytic capabilities
• Number of employees	• Likely number of employees by type by sector across next five years
• Attrition and acquisition rates	• Predictors of attrition, acquisition and performance
• Performance ratings	
• Cost of training	• Drivers of engagement and performance
• Sick days/absenteeism	
• Employee satisfaction	• ROI by training
• Job role standards	• Drivers of absenteeism
• Rules for locating an office in a given city	• Employee engagement, alignment with strategy and agility
• List of competitors likely to be hiring for similar talent	• Job role revisions required to maximize eligible talent availability
	• Best location for new office based on talent costs and availability
	• Best way to compete for talent against competitors by market and talent segment

The rise of analytic capabilities has influenced talent planning and recruiting. Because a significant number of job candidates have posted their résumés digitally, organizations are using technology tools to collect millions of résumés and analyse them to provide sourcing information for individual candidates and groups of candidates. Traditional candidate sourcing approaches are provided by organizations like Jobzology and CEB Talent Assessment, who gather information from individual candidates through surveys and assessments. Based on the responses, the candidates are matched or not matched to the position until the optimal candidate is found. Other technologies (eg Innotrieve, Sunstone Analytics, Wanted Analytics, TalentNeuron) are monitoring trends by gathering data from published sources or screen-scraping the Internet for candidate information. The candidate information can be used to produce the top candidate for an individual job (Innotrieve and Sunstone Analytics). The information can be aggregated to report hiring trends that influence candidate pools (Wanted Analytics) and even predict which markets will provide the best resources in large quantities to sustain a department or business unit (TalentNeuron).

Here's a deeper look at TalentNeuron. This system gathers candidate information from the web and provides an ongoing analysis of the education, experience and backgrounds of resources (unhired candidates and employees) across major metropolitan areas throughout the world. The system creates reports that describe the talent parameters of various cities. An organization can use the system to determine which cities have a critical mass of potential employees with requisite knowledge and skills (eg electrical engineer master's degrees). It also assesses salary, cost of living, demand for candidates and other factors that will help an organization determine if there are enough resources to meet business needs.

All of these systems improve the efficiency and quality of the recruiting process. With them, recruiters can sit with business leaders to discuss labour market intelligence and the availability of talent. TalentNeuron and tools like it presage a day when HR leaders can sit with business leaders empowered by the same capabilities that have transformed supply chain and operations functions to discuss human capital needs, not just as an implication of strategy but rather as a strategic risk that can be managed across time.

CREDIBILITY Seagate's implication-based decision support

In earlier chapters we shared that business leaders often mistrust the data that HR presents to solve business problems. In this case study about Seagate Technology, we examine how the organization built trust with leaders by sharing results and considering consequences – a process that Seagate calls Implication-Based Decision Support. Prior to implementing the implication-based approach, Seagate's leaders were slow to act on the data provided by the HR analytics team. During the transformation, the HR analytics team changed the way it reported results. Instead of providing answers to leadership, they provided implications. Implications are the logical consequences of decisions that leaders might make based on the results of the analysis. This small but substantive change altered leadership's use of the reports provided by the HR analytics team. Here are the three steps that the analytics team used to move toward the implication-based decision support approach.

Make the data consumable

The HR analytics team recognized that a primary barrier to their credibility was the data they provided. Results were often shared in long, cumbersome spreadsheets which were not easily consumed by business leaders. A high quantity of data did not lead to high-quality decisions because important insights were lost in the midst of irrelevant data – and it simply required too much interpretation from both the business partners and the leaders. One area of focus for the team was workforce planning, which was a critical business priority for Seagate, and one where business leaders needed to take more active ownership of decisions.

To move away from the high-quantity and low-quality reporting approach, the analytics team asked a volunteer from one of their internal engineering groups to help them create more compelling and action-oriented visualizations of data. The visualizations contained red and green shading to highlight areas of strength and opportunity. Results were also compared to industry benchmarks. More importantly, dashboards were created and shared with leaders so they could see the distribution of their workforce and how it compared to benchmarks. The HR analytics team found that the data visualizations created a much more tangible platform for constructive conversation and decision making

Enable scenario-based modelling

The next step in the process was to enable leaders to test their hypotheses about the results by using an interactive data visualization tool. Using this tool, leaders adjusted the input data to align with various business scenarios. The tool produced outcomes based on the underlying analytics model, and these outcomes allowed leaders to consider the results and implications of those results. These 'what if' scenarios gave leaders the freedom to test ideas without experiencing real risk. Seagate refers to this approach as 'Leader Self-Discovery'. Instead of making the decision for them, the tool empowers business leaders to make their own decisions based on what the data will look like given their decisions.

Enable decision execution

After business leaders make data-based decisions using the modelling tool, the next step is to execute those decisions. As an example, a leader needs to answer the question, 'What is the optimal workforce distribution for my business unit?' Once the business leader uses the analytics tool and makes what she feels is the right decision, she gathers the HR Business Partners and the HR analytics team to identify working groups and subsequent actions. In this case, the decision is to shift the workforce distribution to include more graduate- and intermediate-level employees. This decision will require involvement from recruiting, L&D and staffing teams. The recruiting team will need to adjust future job requisitions and focus on campus and experienced hiring; the L&D team will need to adjust the curriculum starting with onboarding programmes to fill the gaps for newly hired employees. The staffing team will need to align new hires to new roles. Additionally, the succession planning team will need to get involved too because the changes in hiring will affect promotions and internal mobility. The clarity of action driven from the data-based decisions is helpful in right-sizing talent investments across the enterprise.

The ultimate takeaway from Seagate's work is simply this: the right analytics tool was implemented to empower business leaders to understand their data, test the implications of various choices, and in the end own their talent decisions.

Analytics across the talent lifecycle

As mentioned earlier in this chapter, the HR analytics industry is changing in large part due to the consolidation of talent systems through mergers and acquisitions. Oracle bought Taleo to compete in the talent acquisition market, and SAP bought SuccessFactors to compete in the talent management and learning management arenas. New and innovative technologies also contribute to the advancing capabilities of talent analytics, including a learning records store like Watershed and a candidate culture-fit system like Jobzology.

Recently, CEB acquired several unique technology companies in order to better serve the needs of HR and business leaders. Here is a brief list of those companies and the services they provide:

- **Valtera**
  Conducts employee engagement and other surveys.

- **SHL**
  Assesses candidates for job fit and promotion.

- **PDRI**
  Designs, develops and implements training solutions.

- **Metrics That Matter™**
  Evaluates training and provides benchmarks and reports to determine training effectiveness and next steps for continuous improvement.

- **TalentNeuron**
  Assesses talent populations globally and advises clients where to set up new business units to optimize available resources in geographic locations.

- **Sunstone Analytics**
  Talent acquisition algorithm that helps determine the best candidates for job requisitions.

- **Wanted Technology**
  An analytics system that helps design a better workforce strategy using facts about the talent marketplace.

The value of combining all of these companies under one roof is that clients will eventually be able to gather, analyse and report data from one source. Insights and actions will be easier and faster to achieve. Additionally, clients will have the unique ability to combine data sets along the measurement points in the talent lifecycle and begin to answer questions such as:

- What candidate qualities lead to success on the job?

- Where is the best talent located geographically to set up a regional office?

- Is the training curriculum building capability across the organization?

- Is it more cost effective to hire smart people and train them (build) or hire knowledgeable, experienced resources at a premium (buy)?

- How long will my employees stay, given their current engagement levels?

- Who are the high-potential candidates and how should they be developed?

Individually, each of these questions can be answered by applying one or more of the technologies and services from the organizations mentioned above. The value of combining data sets leads to greater insights. By linking employee engagement scores and turnover results, it is possible to predict who will leave in the next 6, 9 or 12 months. By linking retention and performance measures with candidate profiles from the talent acquisition system, an organization can determine which skills, experience and capabilities produce the most effective, productive and tenured employees. Likewise, such analysis, in combination with some leadership assessments, can produce a short, targeted list of high-potential leaders. As more data becomes available by integrating systems, more questions can be asked and answered with descriptive and predictive analytics.

Conclusion

We began this book with a look at the learning industry and analytics. Throughout, we have shared a variety of ways to apply learning analytics with the intent of answering two questions: 'How effective is training?' and 'How can I improve training if it needs improvement?' The overarching goal for this book was to share best practices that will help organizations measure training with the intent of supporting employee development and in turn improving individual – and ultimately organizational – performance.

When we step beyond learning analytics and begin to consider how to apply analytics to all aspects of talent, we realize the questions are essentially the same: 'How effective are the organization's HR practices?' and 'How can those practices be improved?' Measurement allows us to monitor and manage HR practices with the singular goal of optimizing the performance of the organization.

In the new knowledge economy, why is measurement so important? Talented people are the machines that drive the value of the new economy. If the performance of the organization's greatest asset can be improved, then the organization improves. Measurement is the key to understanding whether HR practices are working and if not, how they can be improved.

Endnotes

1 21 Thomas H Davenport, Jeanne Harris and Jeremy Shapiro (2010) Competing on talent analytics, *Harvard Business Review*, October [online] http://hbr.org/2010/10/competing-on-talent-analytics.

2 Stephen J Dubner (2011) Can car parking direction tell us anything about company morale? Freakonomics [online] http://freakonomics.com/2011/12/30/can-parking-direction-tell-us-anything-about-company-morale/.

3 Stephen J Dubner (2012) The Dilbert Index? A new marketplace podcast, Freakonomics [online] http://freakonomics.com/2012/02/23/the-dilbert-index-a-new-marketplace-podcast/.

4 CEB (2001) Corporate Leadership Council, A New Measurement Mandate: Leveraging HR and Organizational Metrics to Enhance Corporate Performance, internal CEB report.

5 CEB (2008) Corporate Leadership Council, Creating Talent Champions (Volume II) – Best Practices for Engaging Business Leaders in Talent Management, internal CEB report.

6 CEB (2015) CEB Marketing Materials.

7 9 11 15 17 18 19 20 23 CEB (2013) Corporate Leadership Council, The Analytics Era: Transforming HR's Impact on the Business, internal CEB report.

8 PwC (2012) 15th Annual CEO Survey, PwC [online] /www.pwc.com/ en_GX/gx/ceo-survey/pdf/15th-global-ceo-survey.pdf.

10 CEB (2013) Business Barometer, internal CEB report.

12 13 22 24 CEB (2013) Global Labor Market Survey, internal CEB report.

14 16 Jac Fitz-enz (2010) *The New HR Analytics: Predicting the economic value of your company's human capital investments*, AMACOM, New York, NY.

Access to the CEB resources cited in this book is limited to members. For information about membership, please contact CEB's Member Support Centre at CEB.Support@cebglobal.com or +1-866-913-2632.

INDEX

Note: page numbers in *italic* indicate figures and tables.